AND/OR

poems by

Bob King

Finishing Line Press
Georgetown, Kentucky

AND/OR

Copyright © 2025 by Bob King
ISBN 979-8-89990-194-2 First Edition
All rights reserved under International and Pan-American Copyright Conventions. No part of this book may be reproduced in any manner whatsoever without written permission from the publisher, except in the case of brief quotations embodied in critical articles and reviews.

Publisher: Leah Huete de Maines
Editor: Christen Kincaid
Cover Art: "Cosmic Blast" (2003, Mixed Media on Paper, 12" x 12") by Jessica Jones
Author Photo: Bridget C. King
Cover Design: Elizabeth Maines McCleavy

Order online: www.finishinglinepress.com
also available on amazon.com

Author inquiries and mail orders:
Finishing Line Press
PO Box 1626
Georgetown, Kentucky 40324
USA

Contents

I.
This Might Be the Spring She Finally Eats Our Lilac Tree 1
Assume Brilliance 3
The Precision Test's Success 8
When the Atlantic Ocean is Gone in 170 Million Years, Where Are You Going to Fish? 10
They Were Only Invented in 1947, But There Are Now More Transistors on Earth Than There Are Leaves on Trees 13
In Australia, Fast Zombies Are Called Zoombies 15
Rules Are Rules—Until Necessity Intercedes 17
Time & Rockets & Opposites 19
Stephen Jay Gould's Peripatetic Circus 20
Of the First 40 Pilots for Air Mail, Only 9 Didn't Crash & Die ... 22

II.
Chez Jean-Paul: A Three-Star Michelin Journal of Poetry & Pâté Can Suck It 27
It's Not That I Fear Seeing a Ghost, But That I Fear Not Seeing One When Everyone Else Does 29
Mothers of America! Please Let Your Children Come Visit Cleveland! ... 30
I Went to a Cake Shoppe Specifically Because It Was Called SLICES, But They Only Sold Whole Cakes 35
The Night I Met Reincarnated Andy Warhol at Bonnie's Bar & Grill in Fairview Park, Ohio 37
Promise Adventure 38
Bomb City 39
Situation: There's a Pint of Ben & Jerry's in Your Freezer. How Many Nights Does It Last? 40

III.
Global Flavor Riot 43

IV.
When I Finally Began Talking to Myself In Sir David Attenborough's Voice 61
Wax Management 62
The Opposite of Anthropomorphic 63
The Age Where I Need to Take a Photo & Then Zoom In, In Order to Read the Fine Print 64

Because the Weather Changes 65
Think About All the Things You're Not Thinking About 66
I'm Late to It, but Here's a Review of James Cameron's Humongous,
    Gigantic Blockbuster, *Avatar: the Way of Water* (2022) 67
When Will You Stop Trying to Live Up to the Length of Your Own
    Shadow? 68
A Self-Perpetuating Cycle of Self-Perpetuation 69
The Time I Brought a Vase Half-filled with Water to Bed 70

    V.

On Becoming My 75-Year-Old Mother's Medical Marijuana Plug 73
Sometimes You Don't Know You're in a Bubble Until It Pops 75
Terminal Uniqueness 77
Anxiety Mascot 79
It's Magic, When Folks Don't See the Science Behind It 81
Everyone is Walking Along—Floating Along—& You're the One with
    a Stone in Your Shoe 82
Sofia the Flying Telescope 83
Ignorance of the Present 85
Burning Birds & Fiery Jets: Mayday Mayday Mayday is French for
    Help Me 86
The Archeology of the Ampersand 91

    VI.

There's Documented Evidence of Telegraph Operators in the Distant &
    Almost Completely Isolated Operation Stations of the American
    Southwest Falling in Love, Despite the Century Beginning With 18,
    the Tumbleweeds, the Single Iron Wire, Poles Impersonating Cacti,
    Dots, Dashes, Omissions, Hesitations, False Starts, & At-First-
    Unobvious-Yet-Still-Horrific Anti-Indigenous Propaganda 95
Well, Well, Well… As If It Isn't the Consequences of My Own Actions ... 97
I Always Thought That Elton John Song Went, "Hold Me Closer, Tony
    Danza." 98
Like Frogs Around a Pond 99
How to Cultivate Political Propaganda 100
How Often We Store Our Memories Outside Our Minds 102
Mnemonic Device for the Periodic Table of Elements 104

Notes, Acknowledgments, & Gratitude For And/Or 107

For Mom & Dad

And for Bridget, Annie, Coco, & Izzy

I.

This Might Be the Spring She Finally Eats Our Lilac Tree

Anatomically, lilac trees carry their lilac
stress & lilac anxiety in their lilac scent
releases, just as you might in your neck
or limp-laced iliac crest, or she in her jaw
clenching & teeth grinding, or me aback
my throat, one slick black ball swelling
& contracting, depending on the predator
near, not unlike the eastern savanna's
Acacia trees slow-releasing their ethylene
stenches as a giraffe tower approaches,
& in the distance, the hills across the valley
very much look like white elephants—
*I just meant the colouring of their skin
through the trees.* When the measure of
a tree is how comfortable you feel around,
under, or inside it is little different from
the measure of a person. Trees keep their
private parts hidden, & outside of a couple
springtime weeks, there's no possible way
they could be confused with a confessional
poet, though Anne Sexton's Mercy Street
no doubt is lined with lilacs & Peter Gabriel's
version is best served with a healthy dose
of lilac clusters about your face, bunches
of drupelets still sprinkled with droplets
from a misty springtime rain, a rustling
blue plastic grocery bag filled with more
plastic grocery bags, a playground ball pit
filled with endless balls & endless pits,
a science fair project molecule where all
the glittery atoms shed their Styrofoam
dust, shed their variegated hues of purple,
violet, plum, periwinkle, or lavender.
Amethyst or orchid—can we really define
one flower with another flower, one flower
with a gemstone or seashell? A bumblebee
coated & drunk on the burrs of pollen &
burrs of pollen Velcroed to burrs of pollen,
backlit with fuzzy bokeh & Impressionistic

Monet purple clouds with only the occasional
highlight of precision, much like life. Much like
life, the composition of X is often a collection
of many mini-X's, for better or worse,
as when one chlorine scent often carries
a stronger chlorine scent when the community
pool is most in dire need of disinfecting.
Stained glass inside stained glass, ice inside
ice, or in your book, your match always
in danger of lighting the tightly clustered other
matches, sparks into a conflagration,
& a simultaneous desire for & escape from
social distancing protocols. Evolutionarily,
organisms smell for a very precise reason,
& that reason is often survival, or survival
as sacrifice for salvation through another,
conscious decision or not. *Water Lilies*
composed of too many delicate brushstrokes
to count, as when a mother gives birth,
her infinite infant daughter is already
carrying inside her the seeds of the birth
mother's future granddaughter. When will
you realize that everything you love
you don't need to consume, but there's
still a revolution inside you, & likely inside
that, more revolutions, as if pomegranates,
as if some mystical & dreamlike magical
escape into the nighttime embrace of that
delicious Flowering Judas tree: *She pictures
the broken glass, pictures the steam / she
pictures a soul / with no leak at the seams.*
Everything needn't leak or bleed into
or be because of you. This isn't about you.
It's about her. Or the Sexton inside her,
or the Sexton inside her, or the Sexton
inside her. And as much as you may
not like it, it's still her choice, her freedom
to release her perse-hued scent. Or not.

Assume Brilliance

By how much would your life change if
fire instantly vanished from the planet
& we couldn't ever make more? A paradox
is that as industrialization advances, even
though it doesn't seem so—cough-cough—
fewer & fewer acres burn every year
(look it up; it's true), & we actually need to
burn more, in the careful & thoughtful way
indigenous families once did, in the way
woodlands once actually appreciated.
I mean from the Canadian arboreal forests
to our toast, we're really good at burning things.
We're really good at not dialing-in anything
precisely: history, kitchen counter appliances,
paleontology, emotions. If I give you a femur,
can you build a model of the full organism?
If I give you an ancient lump of charcoal,
can you give me a geologic time stamp,
a picture of a family, together feasting
around the neighborhood hearth? You
know, that's why, during our get-togethers
& fancy cocktail parties we all still mostly
gather in kitchens, granite islands & elaborate
centerpieces replacing daily survival as
the real centerpiece of this weird existence.
Biomass to whale oil lamps to Bic lighters,
almost everything today is a potential
firestarter with the number one question:
how do we contain it once we make it?
Think about how many open flames
you see in your daily life & how cities
are now specifically engineered as a series
of fireplaces, fireplaces inside fireplaces,
containers inside larger containers so
we don't see any flames at all anymore,
so we can contain all possible flames,
save the Bath & Body Works 3-wick candles
& occasional mystical sandalwood incense....
do you ever look inside your furnace?

Hot water heater? Tell me about your pilot
lights or patio grill with fancy side burner
or space heater or stovetop or air fryer
or dryer or even your AC unit. Tell me
about your well-placed extinguishers
& detectors & fire walls & escapes & ladders
& even the little silver snuffer Grandma Mac
passed down just for you. Every fire you
don't see in an urban setting is a problem
already solved. From cauldrons to steam
engines to locomotives to space shuttles
to every automobile that's ever existed.
The Camry, with its plucky little get up
& go, the top seller ever, is nothing more
than a finely engineered spark machine.
After all, fire is only 500 million years old,
only purposefully created & contained
for about the last 2 million, & yet, recently,
even if it's not the best time to be *Homo sapiens,*
it's definitely the best time to be fire.
Homo flagrans. Like *Homo hydrocarbons,*
most of what we desire is one spark away
from what we feel we can become, one
equation reactant away from what we feel like
we were always meant to be, & yet it's more
likely that we've become the tool of our tools,
whether it's as a congregation to the pastor
of trapped-between-the-rocks crude oil,
or the new shells for the microplastics
that now comprise our sewer systems
& one giant interconnected ocean—like
double helixes, all our plumbing eventually
connected, if/when you really stop & think
about it, plumbing inside plumbing,
the whole world one giant Rube Goldberg
of drains & dams & locks & pipes & tubes
& overflows & catch basins. Or perhaps
the microscopic minerals that make
the transistors that now make up AI,
or maybe even when obligation to help
those on the margins becomes a twisted

attempt to place more people on the margins.
When isn't more always hidden inside
more? This fire, tool, the ultimate catalyst,
the ultimate interactive technology, more like
an ox than a hammer because when we're
finished with it for the day, it doesn't just
nicely rest in its holster on clearly outlined
pegboard in the garage. Tools, like emotions,
often surprisingly invert, though it shouldn't
at all be a surprise. News flash: life can exist
without fire, but fire can't exist without
the organic world. We go away, so does it,
save the lightning strikes that do far less
damage than the spectacle would have you
believe. The median can't exist without
the margins, & yet you're most likely to find
your fire in those very same margins. Despite
all this fuel, oxygen, & heat, we are, as a species,
empowered yet immature forces of nature.
Only in this biosphere as we know it
can we take apart what photosynthesis
puts together. *Oh, don't mind him, he's just
a combustible personality* becomes blind
excuse-making instead of accountability.
Grow up, Devonian Period. We're no longer
fishes, & maybe they were onto something
when they called the hobby *fishing* instead of
catching. In this way, we're very much like
hydrocarbons—there's nothing more that we
desperately want than to burn. Why can't this
process turn us into something that instead
wants to learn? And now, today, what's really
important to you, what makes or breaks your
entire weekend, is whether or not you get to
sit in the lowly-lit corner booth you most love
down at the corner pub, as if safety from
an imagined mafia hit is the real reason
you want your back to the wall. Bro,
the Neanderthals aren't conspiring
against you, your conspiracy theory
not affirmed just because you got a detail

or two accidently correct. So, here's what
you do: on the way home, you insist
that you walk streetside of the sidewalk,
you stop calling your spouse *her* & instead
use her name & then you insist Deborah walks
on the house-shop-building side, mostly under
the awnings, just in case the Middle Ages come
screaming back & chamber pots once again start
flying out the windows. I'm talking to you, you
who's brain seems to be conspiring against
your own tranquility, happiness, success.
You who is so used to fear in your passenger
seat that you don't even recognize fear sitting
in your passenger seat, smug & ginger-headed
& mercurial. Do you mind rolling up your
window, as I'm getting the wind's hollow-bass
hum that feels like it's going to fan the flames,
to suck out my eardrums, the low bass drum
thrumming in my chest like another 3am
panic attack where I think everything is
burning. Heat, drought, peat smoke,
& sparkplugs—just another Promethean
sidequest gone terribly wrong because
we've always been terrible at anticipating
side effects, & yet still, like happiness,
we're often better off living in the side
effects than we are consuming ourselves
with combustible goals. He not only gave
us fire, was shackled to a rock, but he also
tried to give us hope, a torch, birthday
candles & songs, families coming together,
& soon enough, if you're not really careful,
if you don't start paying attention,
you might become the mayor of a North
American town that no longer exists,
a mighty Ozymandian empire of ash,
a Johnny Cash empire of dirt, so maybe learn
the history, tighten the lids on the gas cans
of humility & doubt, as you have more
of those than you'll ever possibly consume,
& then relax, give yourself some grace,

& choose to live here, not back then,
& not under the burning tempest there
in the distance of the Pyrocene. If even
the sparks can possess the confidence
of a full-blown firestorm, so can you.
If you too often see yourself as a sapling
& sometimes forget that you're a giant
sequoia, you're still a giant sequoia, with
as much unseen depth as skyward height—
you're flame resistant & always much better
off being an active participant than you are
merely being a passive witness.

The Precision Test's Success

For Connie

Depends upon whether or not your machine
can make other machines, with the accuracy,
precision, & elegance of a ghostly Rolls-Royce,
even if Royce got shafted by Rolls on the
naming rights, even if not quite et al'd—
when hasn't the money throttled
the mechanic? It happens all the time
with questions, this test birthing another
test, but can your poetry make other
poetry, your body other bodies, your
teaching not students, but other teachers?
Or are you only a consumer? Can you be
very accurate with your arrows-conclusions,
but not at all precise, as when you're not
even close to bullseye, far-flung & nowhere
near inspiring a new industrial revolution?
Could you give a flip about being a boring
machine that hollows out cannons with
exactitude, no accidental naval deaths
on your hands, or are you ridiculously
consumed with what might be considered
canon & what's enchanting about being
on the margins—rusted, pock marked,
perhaps fluking into success, even if
the occasional one unexpectedly explodes—
very unlike Westinghouse, Edison, or Ford?
Wilkinson, Maudslay, or Bramah? Sure,
Eli Whitney's famous gin was marvelous
if we forget about what it really helped
fuel in that Antebellum South, if we forget that
he was a con artist-slash-terrible
engineer when it came to gun production,
his damage already done, as damage is
more likely than not always a child to
damaged parents. Would you prefer
to be handmade or assembly lined?
Shakespeare was great & all, but

dude never even used a dictionary,
even though now all dictionaries spawn
other dictionaries, but English dictionaries
hadn't even been invented yet, & to be fair
he didn't make other Shakespeares either,
but did make love test after love test, only
occasionally kings, but kings don't always
produce other kings, but almost always fools
are guaranteed to produce other fools.
That's wild to me, the no dictionaries
bit—only a few usage pamphlets. But
it also makes complete sense. Like
electricity. Or photosynthesis. Or that
we even have names for chloroplast,
electrochemical gradients, mitochondrial
machines, proteins, or that a fungus is
the Earth's heaviest organism, or that
now we can take language in reverse,
crisply define a process like ATP synthase:
$ADP + Pi + 2H+out \rightleftharpoons ATP + H2O + 2H+in$
Does all mill grist produce more grist,
or if we roll this stone long enough
will we truly produce something new,
or maybe only discover contentment in
the recycled, reconstituted, resurrected
zombie moldy old? Does every stockyard
slaughterhouse get counterbalanced
by a slow-moving conveyor belt that'll
even bring back Lazarus? Are we deemed
or doomed or both only to ever be precise
to ourselves? Hey Mary Shelley, please
pass me the calipers, a wrench, & that
asterisk-impersonating screwdriver,
I found a glitch inside another glitch,
one thought not inside another, but
more like simultaneously occurring,
like lightning, inspiration, like how
one love can't produce another love,
except in the precisely accurate &
simultaneously messy & inarticulate
love you're able to provide to all three
of your daughters at once at once at once.

When the Atlantic Ocean is Gone in 170 Million Years, Where Are You Going to Fish?

Or dip your toes at the surf's edge because
that's right, she's about 50% through her
lifespan, always to-us-like-us in midlife
crisis & there's nothing we can do about it,
& it'll be strange when the New Jersey
Boardwalk, with its honky-tonk glaring
purple neon stolen from the Romans
stolen from the Phoenicians stolen from
the royal mollusks, becomes the new
front porch in West Africa because Africa
is where front porches were invented
certainly not discovered before 12 million
slaves got poached from her cradle by t
hose Dutch, English, Portuguese, Spanish,
Belgians, & hey, you certainly don't get
a pass, Carolinians, with your reintroduction
to where it all began, Lucy not Eve,
you heavy-accented Massachusetts
longshoremen now where the Canary
Islands used to be. It's not just the re-
spooled spools of outdated telegraph
wires laid like stitches across the north,
across the ersatz under water Rocky
Mountains, across the thank-god
level-best full fathom five plateaus
before Tesla & Marconi came along
& solved that countries-as-introverts
problem that wasn't a problem because
just because their culture isn't your culture
doesn't mean it's savagery. It's not like
we can simply pack it all up & take it all
with us. This isn't a vacation or a holiday.
Not just a conquest or consolation prize.
It's not just humble Leif Erikson with his
Newfoundland encampment without
making a federal case federal holiday
out of it, unlike that Genoan sailor more
a product of the church-led masterful

marketing campaign than any authentic
discovery or invention. It's not just the oil
spills & microplastics & not at all, not even
a little microplastic because there's
nothing micro about regrouping remaking
into a giant polypropylene continent,
because even though we can't feel it,
all the continents are moving in a way
that makes you realize what's significant
isn't, & they've never stopped & will
once again Pangea, a Tierra del Fuego
lighthouse puzzle shape shifting, as if
that family-together holiday project
of standard cut glossy carboard pieces
on a well-lacquered dining room table,
& sure you all sat & talked & completed
the border with your wine & classical
music in the background as if you all
could be all cultured & thus forget about
the world's bluntness for one two three
a few evenings, but you all eventually
returned to your lives & the Patagonian
lighthouse, as if on its own, as if fate is
really a thing, will slip past India & back
into a slot where Americans used to
base in Okinawa, US containment policy
finally totally shot, a glorious feat of
plate tectonic gymnastics that perhaps
only a distant grandkid will be around
to witness, & who knows what DNA
will look like then, maybe that child is
part me, part you, part Neanderthal,
part robot, AI, cyborg, or ChatGTP.
Did you know there's a creek in Montana
called the Atlantic Creek because that
creek is part of where her mother or
would it be daughter ocean begins,
8,000 foot Triple Divide Peak, Montana
to a sandy steep southeastern slope
to another creek to the Marias River
to the Missouri River to the Mississippi

to the Gulf of Mexico to the Atlantic,
to the depths & those unrecovered
bodies & treasures & global sins &
this convergence is why introverts
often ask themselves why they have
to speak up when it'd be just as easy
for extroverts to shut the hell up for
once. Where will all that unclaimed
lost gold go, Discovery Channel salvage
divers from dying reefs from pirates
from Conquistadors from Montezuma
from when aren't we narcissistic enough
to think we pulled ourselves up by our
own bootstraps, the watery memorial
of the *Titanic* & U-boat victims not just
sunk, but sunk again, forever folded
inside the Earth's crust, as if we're
kneading bread dough, keep folding it
inside itself, & fold & fold & fold until
it achieves just the exact consistency
you're looking for, & sure go ahead,
go ahead & add all the exotic fruits
& spices you want, & bake at 350 until
the end of time. Sure, I'll say I'm not
irritated by *waves arms broadly,* but
the truth may be otherwise. But this isn't
an elegy. It's a recipe for gratefulness.

They Were Only Invented in 1947, But There Are Now More Transistors on Earth Than There Are Leaves on Trees

And there are an estimated 3 trillion trees,
& are we counting needles as
leaves or not? We cool leaving out pine
& hemlock & spruce, Norwegian & blue
& any other kind of not yet named or
invented spruce? French Guiana leads the
way with 20,226 trees per person, thanks
Google, & Suriname is the highest
percentage of covered-by-trees, with your
country way down the rankings, so don't
even bother looking, because your old
Cold War enemy is #1 when we're
talking sheer number of trees inside
her borders, & you're right we haven't
even yet contemplated the leaves on
the sugar maples, Japanese maples,
crabapples, dogwoods, birch, walnut,
chestnuts-before-the-blight, oak, & elm on
your street alone. And if you can't
even win your street, what business do you
have in the local, regional, state, or federal
level? I've been to Monaco with
its 0% forested land, its royal state of
arboreal undress, but there's a cool
story about the prince there leaving
a rose graveside for his gone-too-soon
graceful princess every day after her
death until he had her statuesque beauty
captured in bronze & named a federal
rose garden in her honor. Would you
do that for your beloved? The roses?
The petals? Do you believe in soulmates
that much? Do you believe in anything
that much? In the span of 76 years, an
average lifetime, mankind is capable of
inventing something, shrinking it X fold,
 getting so many inside your phone, TV,
clinging to its anachronistic culture radio,

other TV, TVs the kids don't even watch
anymore, phones, cameras, desktops
& laptops & extra monitors, not to mention
headphones & speakers & appliances
& gizmos & doodads & whatchamacallits,
& who isn't building their own rocket
ship in their backyard? Another wannabe
cosmic explorer billionaire, & look
I know the Robber Barons were awful, but
at least they left libraries & theaters
& appreciated art & now you wake up
& don't even know what you believe in
because you've been so fixated on cutting
burning deforesting all the good others
are trying to do in the world & when
are you going to realize all the tech
in the world isn't going to make
communication communion any
easier if you can't at least—like
one quaking leaf on a windblown
locust tree in flower—make yourself
vulnerable every now & then?

In Australia, Fast Zombies Are Called Zoombies

Likely, that's not true. But whether
it's the truth or not, truth is always
mostly hope that the settled version
of things remains settled. The person
who wronged you once remains wrong
forever. The dead remain dead, the buried,
buried, even down under Down Under
because the people who threaten our
assumptions we then need to classify
as absolutely mad, as if a necessary act
of self-preservation. What's nuts to me
is that in-the-shows-in-the-movies all
the zombies are either especially slow
or *World War Z* wicked fast. Amblers
or speedsters. They don't account for
the fact that when the virus or bacteria or
fungus took root & spread faster
than a-bug-a-thought-a-meme, some
of those pre-zombies were very likely
sedentary: some sofa-bound & not even
trying anymore to stave off the mushy
lump of the middle-aged dad bods. Some
like the kind smiling lady in the oversized
straw hat with sunflower emblem &
sunglasses who neighborhood strolls
nodding & peace-signing everyone
every day, as if the calendar never
changes. And some, training for their
next 5k or half marathon. You never
see the undead all moving at their own
pace—wheel-chairing (what zombie flick
ain't ableist?) or wandering or limping
or sprinting, chafed nipples bleeding
or hamstrings seizing or heck even
falling off—toward the finish line
of their next victims. Some happy
& entirely content to be part of the
slow-moving-cheerleader procession.
When did everyone become one thing?

When did everything begin to remind
you of something else? When will
we arrive at the original antecedent,
the prime mover, initial explosion,
as if truth isn't constantly evolving
in a series of small mutations, delicious
& gnawed right down to the bone? In
this family, as in most, we've the gift
of speech, but we won't use it for
the things most vital, generational
reticence at its best. Do you know
most zombies would kill to be able to
communicate how they've been hurt,
the wounds & scars of youth they still
lug into their absurdist present? Do you
realize the ridiculous good in the world
squirrels, zombified or not, could do
with speech, unfurling their treetop
wants & desires, fears & fantasies,
traumas & aspirations to do some
good with that amazing power? And
yet, there you remain, sullen & arms
crossed on the couch, determined not
to talk about how you're falling apart
& for some reason ashamed that you
can't reassemble all on your own?
Healing was never meant to be
a solitary sport. And so, this spring
all the tulips are wearing our castoff
N-95s, dirty roadside empathy, but
the daffodils are not. This is the rule
of time. We exist for others, & then
we don't.

Rules Are Rules—Until Necessity Intercedes

Because we really wanted to know what
makes her tick, we recently
drilled a hole 2 miles deep into Earth
over the San Andreas Fault & one of
the engineers on the project, Neal,
suggested we get a really long wick
from ACME & light this sucker as if
a stink bomb tossed into the BOYS john
so they'd have no choice but to cancel
the fast-approaching final exam. In the
least, we'd get a recess they weren't
planning to give. That Neal. There's
one in every group, am I right?
I mean, we know the fault is there,
we know there are faults in us, like
maybe a cracked heel bone, & wouldn't
this be like using your DeWalt Hammer
Drill to inspect that fracture instead of
an X-Ray machine? It's like we invent
slowly, then all at once, then begin to
misuse or even abuse or forget those
tools. We're always forgetting what
got us here & what we're doing to
hasten our exits. Someone else suggested
we keep going, we drill the whole way
through: we lick our lips & squint our
eyes & thread a fishing line through,
adding a cool, if overused, paisley bead
to the ultimate friendship bracelet,
perhaps for Zeus' fast-approaching
birthday, even if we've lost track
of how old he is. Despite what Neal
suggested, the deepest hole drilled
into the ground was not named
Your Mother, said in a terrible
Scottish accent, which led to other
terrible Sean Connery & Alex Trebek
& Will Ferrell impressions. When
impressions supersede the original,

when we've dreamt of, but not yet
invented a sustainable replacement
we only get comic caricatures—where
did you come from, Burt Reynolds
in an enormous cowboy hat? Yes, we
understand it's funny because
it's oversized, outsized this prized
jewel of chemistry, geology, &
astrophysics, but back to what
I was saying—the deepest hole
drilled into the crust only went
about 7½ miles in, & the plan was
to get a giant syringe to suck out
all the good carbon filling. Or was it
to inject some blueberry ganache?
What if Earth's entire crust, the entire
25 miles deep of it, 25 miles deep
times the circumference containing
all the known life in the universe,
25 miles of rock & water, sand
& plants, people & their particulates,
was replaced with blueberries? How
many do you suspect we'd need?
And while you're at it, can you
also calculate what exactly necessity
herself needs in order to intercede?

Time & Rockets & Opposites

Go home, Yank. We do not like your kind here,
said the hotel clerk in Central London.
To be fair, I requested a new room,
one that didn't smell like the NYC Subway.
During the Blitz, where the bombs fell
was as random as life gets. Or ends.
Hotel brick dust on too many bowlers.
Apple in front of a face in a painting
only 5 years later. The thing is, with
the V-2's, you often heard them after
they landed & if they landed on you,
well then you never heard them,
time's inversion surprising you with its
complete ability to surprise after the fact.

Stephen Jay Gould's Peripatetic Circus

My best carnival trick is noticing the elephant
in the room in whatever room I'm in, feeling
the weight of the expectations or taboos,
as they shift depending on the audience or
type of big top tent. James Joyce said to pay
attention to the small things, given the absurdity
& brevity of all the other things, so Gould took
that to mean dinosaurs, & it didn't bother him
that most people who ever lived never knew
that dinosaurs ever even existed. What bothers
you that others don't even know about? Yes, take
that both ways it's meant, both in the sense
of what's bothering you that you simply can't
ever share AND what's bothering you that
others aren't even aware of? The thingness
of the thing, & you're right, there's probably
at least a third meaning that no one on the planet
has yet discovered. Have you yet allowed yourself
to consider the short- & long-term benefits of
seeing a therapist? Have you yet discovered
the absolute immensity of the work it takes
to get others to care? And when you really want
something, you rub the lamp furiously, but
the more furiously you rub the lamp,
the smaller the Genie appears to be.
So we keep saying, If I can just make it t
o the next paycheck, the weekend, heck
the way things are going, if I can just make it
to 5 o'clock, I'm going to reward myself with
a cocktail & deep fried appetizers. Hey Pal,
says the surly patron at the bar's end, & he
definitely looks worse for wear, in his smoky
5 o'clock shadow, but he's also somehow
made it to 5 o'clock somehow, & you want
to tell him that & to call you Bert because
you heard that Herbert Hoover's closest pals
called him Bert, but then he might think that
you're being too Sesame Street, but you're not,
you're really being earnest, & you want to say,

Look friend, like Bert's Great Depression,
I am taking too much heat, or I am giving myself
too much heat for what are clearly extenuating
global conditions, from this economy to the peace
treaty that didn't work out as planned, reparations
causing resentment & instability rather than
the accountability they were meant to provide.
Weather is daily changing. Climate is more
progressive & longer term, but both have
a bearing on the moods we're in, & somewhere-
everywhere, something-everything is on fire,
but sure, it's fine for today, for right now, if
you go ahead & open up to a stranger, yes,
yes it is yes it is yes it is, & still yes it is.

Of the First 40 Pilots for Air Mail, Only 9 Didn't Crash & Die

They all died eventually—after the fact
spoiler alert—just not from an airplane
engine conking out mid barnstorming
barrel roll, or from the cross-country
Burbank to Cleveland Bendix Trophy Race.
Yes, Cleveland of all places, once fly-to
rather than flyover country. Cleveland
with these roads & landscapes & stitchwork
of seasonal colors I daily travel, once flown
to & trod by—actually on purpose—
Earhart, Turner, & Lindberg, as if
them being on/over/above the geography
a century ago makes me special for
being in it now. Credit or blame,
creation or destruction, reason for
or from nothingness. *Well, I started out*
Down a dirty road / Started out all alone
And the sun went down / As I crossed the hill
And the town lit up / The world got still
I'm learning to fly / But I ain't got wings
Coming down / Is the hardest thing.
When those early pilots got lost,
which was often, given the lack of
technology, beacons, GPS, they'd
start following the long railroad tracks,
the red barn roofs painted with small
town locations, Jesus Saves & Adult Bookmart
billboards not yet part of the landscape,
but when you want to start any industry,
auto or airline, religion or pornography,
the industry of poetry or emotions, start it with
a race, make it a competition, build
the spectacle, the biplane pylon races out
over Lake Erie drawing more of a crowd than
the pro baseball team. *Spetakkel* is
the Norwegian quality of rambunctiousness,
noisy & uproarious, & oh lord they were
rambunctious, those early flygirls,
breaking all the barriers, norms, gender

roles & expectations, Earhart & Thaden,
Nichols & Elden, Gunderson & Klingensmith.
Sprezzatura is the Italian word cavalierly
coopted by the Cavalier Poets, trying to
make their precise & studied poems seem
dashed-off & nonchalant, as if they
could be prototypes for Amelia—or me. From
her plane, from her chrome yellow
Friendship, Electra in her Electra, tempting the
fates or seeking justice for existence,
from Earth's curvature, poetry in the sky,
a takeoff, updraft, that feeling of up up
upness when you know you're onto
something new & strange & wonderful,
the act of creation as uplifting as getting
your hands grease or dirt or gasoline
covered, a social worker on the ground,
a driver, auto mechanic, dump truck
operator & Canadian Red Cross nursemaid
for those Great War survivors with their
amputations & amputated spirits,
shell shocked before PTSD was named,
forever an imprint on no-makeup Amelia,
their morality tales prompting her quest
to wring every zest from this great big
orange, & even the mountains grew
humble in her fleeting presence, our
fleeting presences, & who can't bend
landscape & aeronautics, physics
& engineering, desire & geology,
to our will? Who can't romanticize
navigation & crashes & dead stick landings
& successfully dumping in the Hudson
decades before Captain Sully made
the news & honestly, I don't know how
anyone gets through life without being
a bit romantic. I'm not talking all Shelley
& *Western Wind* & Oh, Western Wind
With living hues and odours plain and hill:
Wild Spirit, which art moving everywhere;
Destroyer and preserver; hear, oh hear!

Okay, so maybe I am a little bit. Maybe
that wind does carry revolution with
its seeds & pollen this way or that
across the Atlantic, & most definitely
it'd be nice forever having our eternal
presence on the wind, the leaves & currents
& wave crests & meadows & overgrown
moss & prayers & incantations & inside
almost every whisper between fathers
& daughters, husbands & wives, lovers
& lovers. How can we not worry about
what we take from or leave for the sky,
this turtle island, this great circle, those
we love the most? The journey & the
destination? The tangible & the
imprecise? All that soaring for the sake
of soaring. She's still flying, you know.
In my mind, she's still flying, out there
flying around, among & through clouds,
stitching them back together as quickly
as she splits them open, the comforting
infinities of trade & cross, prevailing &
westerlies, polar & doldrums, & yeah,
she's still air-cooled, dead reckoning,
& still navigating all of us to a place,
a place of wonder that we'll know,
we'll surely know, when we get there.

II.

Chez Jean-Paul: A Three-Star Michelin Journal of Poetry & Pâté **Can Suck It**

First, from the elegant Online Exclusives
menu, gimme a twist-cap-to-go bottle of
Tips for Getting Out of Flight Mode as I know
more straw-sucked Diet Coke won't help
as it'll keep my BP & electric skin RPMs
redlined, but it tastes just so dang festive,
& these dang escargot sweats don't have
an off switch, but it's still worth wearing
the collared shirt I look best in, isn't it?
[Checks hair part in the rearview mirror.]
Do I belong in this lane? Does anyone? It's
almost always easier to believe what you
already think than it is to change your mind,
but come on, light, aesthetic, season, epoch…
change. Please. Maybe drive off to the museum,
next? A symphony in your earbuds, gentle rain
on the plant-covered patio, the remnants
of culture in carefully curated plexiglass
boxes on pedestals, cameras & heat-sensitive
pressure sensors keeping a careful watch,
& we'll need a taut but supple nighttime
acrobat to navigate the invisible indivisible
lasers protecting the immortality via
objectification, an entire civilization
reduced to *they made this, so we'll choose
to remember only them* & maybe stop being
so quick to place people on said pedestals,
mythmaking at its carved marble worst.
Will people's need for mysteries & legends
ever allow them to fully accept reality?
Maybe we should check the victor's
Language Arts grades & ethical sensibilities
before we allow him to write all the history?
Where's a gruntled adjunct professor when you
need one? He may have made cool stuff,
but he, like Ty Cobb or Robert Bleeping Frost,
was a prick to everyone in his life, sacrificing a
life well-lived for suspect fame afterwards,

as if anyone's goal in life is to end up under
glass in The Natural History Museum instead
of The Museum of Awful Drive Thru Poetry,
as if curating *I do this, I do that* is a less than
reputable career. When exactly did this
airy cloche morph into impermeable
Museum World? One friend a thief,
the other a Ben Stiller lookalike ersatz
security guard. Another friend's nickname
is Number Two because of his love of Ohio's
Pencil Museum. Erase, blow away the pink
shavings, & graphite-scratch-in that
it's actually a Pencil Sharpener Museum
that he adores—better to be the honer
than the honed. Besides, I don't know
where the actual Pencil Museum is, despite
the ease of Googling, just as I can know
where the Peanut Butter Museum is (PA)
without desperately needing to know
where the Jelly Museum is, though I do
admire his sticktoitiveness, even if it's his
poetry I can't shake loose from the roof of
my mouth. Of course, there must be one—
 mouth to feed or another fulcrum
for the teetertotter—as we always want
balance, a neatness to spousal condiments,
as we're exceedingly uncomfortable
with aloneness, with lack of explanation,
but then again, maybe we're all too content
with the banality of elitism, the suck of
a lemon. Y'all got those warm chocolate
& cinnamon-sugar sprinkled churros
on the menu yet?

It's Not That I Fear Seeing a Ghost, But That I Fear Not Seeing One When Everyone Else Does

As we try to figure out whether we're
better off being controlled than being
controlling, I can't slam on my brakes
fast enough to avoid the male Northern
Cardinal checking on his still & silent
fledgling on the new asphalt on Route 43
just outside Twin Lakes & before I know it,
he's somersaulting over my grill, hood,
windshield, luggage rack, & morphs into
a rearview mirror blurry red dandelion
puff & tumbles into the roadside gulley,
back into the uncrafted design of things.
While I may not believe anymore, I've
vast respect for those who do, those who
can set aside the sins of the institution,
still controlled by those same men,
in order to find comfort within the walls
of the very same institution where even
the heads-bowed-whispered-word abuse
has-like-wine deliberately become diluted—
the way the spring sunlight filters through
the stained glass panes still offering some
some small semblance of-hope-of-truth
or maybe-even-I-don't-quite-know-how
transcendence.

Mothers of America! Please Let Your Children Come Visit Cleveland!

Because look, we didn't set the *entire* river
on fire. And that was so long ago. And now
you can barely smell it. Most of the sulfurous
steel mills have shuttered so sometimes
the sun is actually visible, even if that means
so too is unemployment. Our pro football
team isn't always terrible, & there are
some genuinely great guys on the squad,
not just the domestic abusers, & the studs
will eventually sign bigger contracts & win
a Super Bowl with other teams. Good for them,
right? We're genuinely happy to see others
succeed where we can't. Vicarious victory
mixed with a healthy dose of imposter
syndrome mortared & pestled in a valley of
missed opportunities. But hey, on the bright
side of the ledger, we finally got rid of our
decades-old racist baseball mascot & part
of me never understood why the players,
(money) mostly minorities, *(money)* never
(money) refused to wear that Wahoo crap
(money) & look, many of us do recognize
now that it's definitely not cool to blame
the multitude of victims for the sins of
the master's money. I mean John D. Rockefeller
got his start here & other than the wake
of bloody busted union heads he left at the gates
of his refineries & the fact that there's an entire
board game which memorializes his maniacal
attempt to monopolize, he wasn't too bad.
Not the kind of guy who'd buy you a drink
at the corner public house, like most of us
shot & a beer Clevelanders, but I'm sure
he's got a lot of other things on his gold-plated plate
right now, given his champagne taste
actually coupled with a champagne budget.
Even if all ashes look like ashes & all dust,
dust, & what's it matter anyway because at most,
if we don't gum up the works sooner, this ball

of dirt is only going to be around for another
1.5 billion years. Quantum physics & geologic
time = the great nullifier of all of us. This is
to say, you'll get over it. And we Clevelanders
can keep making excuses for others who don't
need us to make excuses for them because
excuse-making is in our goddamn water.
We're annually nationally ranked for our
cursing prowess, but I'm not sure what
committee decides that. Likely some
looking-down-their-noses-East-Coast-
bitch-ass-motherfuckers. Our basketball
team actually won a ring when our area-
born-&-raised Chosen One chose to leave on
national TV & then reunited, said he
was sorry, groveled back, gave us a ring
that was better than the makeup sex, only
to leave again. Cleveland: *the land of being wanted,
but only for a little while.* But let me assure you
that we're not the jealous or grudge-carrying
type, unless your name is John Elway, Michael
Jordan, Pittsburgh, Baltimore, or that state
up north. Or if you're Irish. Or Italian.
Or Greek. Or Slovakian. Or any number
of other small enclave communities who
hold those grudges almost as well as we
hold our alcohol & penchant for never
quite saying what we really want to say.
If you're into that kind of thing, we do have
an internationally award-winning orchestra
& late-Victorian Age opulent theater district,
even if it's only mostly the out-of-towners
who can afford tickets. Most of us have collars
that are too blue & we sometimes forget how
to tie a tie. The incessantly rumpled suitcoat
& unkempt hairdo of the Senior Senator from
the East Side, who's delightfully well-read
& just progressive enough to still reach both
sides of the aisle, might be our ideal model—
if looks didn't matter for a model & the
downstate conspiracy theorists stayed quiet

in their mother's basements. If you're into
that kind of thing, we're the birthplace of
Rock-n-Roll & the museum has such uplifting
exhibits as John Lennon's glasses he was murdered
in in New York, just off Central Park. Sure, they're
still blood-spattered, but so are most of us,
& like us, they are still pretty damn cool,
if you're into that kind of thing. And our
world renown Natural History Museum
has all kinds of bird skins in an elaborate
dusty cabinet-file system in its dank basement,
& if you know the right person, you can
attend a workshop there, don some latex
gloves & stuff the birds' bellies with cotton,
making them pregnant with meaning again,
filling their eyeholes with more cotton,
nothing but blind dead bird eye whites staring
at you so that you want to handcraft little head
bandannas to make their creepiness a little
less weird, because not all our creeps are
super weird. Sure, like any wanna be metropolis
we've had our share of serial killers, but most
of us want to stay sexy & not get murdered.
Exhibit A: Superman was born here. And Paul
Newman, Tracy Chapman, & Tom Hanks
will testify on our behalf. Life tip: it's always
good to know a few folks who will testify
on your behalf. And we do have a couple
of the top, first-rate health care systems
in the world, even if our history of rust,
pollution, & carcinogens are likely
the main reasons for needing a top hospital
system. Or two. After all, is it really all
that random that a solution to a problem
(i.e., a hospital), would pop up & achieve
popstar fame in an area that doesn't demand
a need for solutions to said problems?
We've an awesome national park & our
Metropark system that forms a green jewel
necklace around the city is rated among
the tops in the nation. True story. Ask any

Clevelander. If/when they aren't busy at
the Christmas house made famous by that
movie that fetishizes a detached but still
kinda kinky light up leg in a fishnet stocking.
Oooh la la. Fra gee lay. Most of us don't think
we talk with accents. *Cuyahoga, you guys.*
You best put your *pop* cans on the *tree lawn*
for recycling, & our overly elaborate
highway system has been under construction
since construction started after the last
world war, & literally everything is
20 minutes away except the airport,
& somehow now everyone in every
neighborhood is now in the landing pattern.
Yes, we can be smug enough that we try
to neighborly talk over the revving engine
of the landing 747 as we share that chat between
mowing crisp spearmint lines into our front
lawns. Small pride in, *Gosh, doesn't the grass
look great this spring?* No yeah sure, I agree,
the team's really got a shot at finally winning
next year. We'll brag on our yards & parks all
day long. Given our obesity rate, we won't actually
use said greenspaces all day long, but hey they sure
do look pretty. We're also superstars on bragging
about what we lack. As in deserts, hurricanes,
earthquakes, elitism, & façades. We're future
Nobel Prize winners at ignoring what brings
us shame, as in almost any difficult conversation,
as in the purposeful repurposing of all those
goddamn parish priest child molesters,
the white flight, the voter repression &
mortgage redlining, & the Hough race riots.
But look, not unlike the t-shirt crowd in the early
bird overcrowded lobby of the Olive Garden,
When you're here, you're family. And family doesn't
always get held accountable. We & we alone
can make fun of our siblings, but don't you
dare try it, unless you want a pow, a sock
right in the kisser, wise guy. Elliot Ness didn't
make a name for himself on our streets by

coincidence. And while most of our college
graduates do, in fact, end up leaving the state,
& while our city planners still haven't figured
out how to take advantage of a waterfront
destination like Chicago, NYC, Paris, London,
or heck most global cities with a port or a river
running through them, & even if our name
literally means *land of things that break apart*,
it's still home, *& I think, by heaven,* our city
as rare, as any she belied with false compare.
So, raise your glasses— don't worry,
we got most of the lead out of the pipes
long ago—to Cleveland! Land of thank-
fucking-god we're still upstream from Detroit.

I Went to a Cake Shoppe Specifically Because It Was Called SLICES, But They Only Sold Whole Cakes

Which is how I decided, as the baker
explained it all to me, to open a FLOWERS
store, but we'd only sell shrubs & trees,
as in pink dogwoods against a navy house,
but then I remembered my cousin Dan
had a plant store already & his orchid
section entailed stepping into getting lost
in a Brazilian rain forest, his broadleaf
tropicals a protector from the slow
pitter patter of the drop, & look there's
a neon frog at your feet. Don't touch it.
Don't lick it. And as I left SLICES,
I stepped into the bodega next door
for some bread, sugar, & milk, only
I found neatly bagged & surprisingly
unsquished loaves of neatly wrapped
Ukrainian wheat fields. A Barbadian
cane plantation to teach a lesson about
sweet tooth fueled empire & conquest
& inhumanity. I found siloed & cartoned
cows lolling on their shelves, anticipating
rain, mooing me toward the curious
chickens on their own shelves made of
red wheelbarrows made of mountains
& environmentally damaging mountain
mining operations, & where did all
these former mountains come from,
& at what cost to progress is progress,
& are those dinosaurs & generations of
compressed plankton where the Vaseline
& shampoos should be? Why thank you,
Stegosaurus, yes, you're right, I am having
a good hair day. And while I have you here,
I must admit, I know it's not my job to fix
everything bad about the world, but jeez,
I never thought that trying would cripple
me-you-it-them-the-conjunction-of-all-of-this
so much, & until it goes extinct & it's not even

close to going extinct, the main ingredients in
cake will always be cake, but also so much more.

The Night I Met Reincarnated Andy Warhol at Bonnie's Bar & Grill in Fairview Park, Ohio

He ordered a margarita in a kitschy plastic cactus glass—of course salted rim—& had the deep- fried perch platter. Weirdly, he skipped the soup, & the whole evening Frida Kahlo sat in the corner, menacingly staring at us, forking her cobb salad to her mouth from a bowl fashioned out of a bedazzled human skull, & honestly, we thought we'd have more company, but Hopper walked in, surveyed the scene, muttered, *Too crowded*, & left. Pollock got booted for again tossing his spaghetti at the wall & we couldn't get Duchamp out of the Men's Room. Lord only knows what he & Mapplethorpe were doing in there. We'll never know why the one patron at bar's end had Billy Joel's "The Downeaster Alexa" on jukebox repeat or why Dali's spoons bent, wilted, melted, while O'Keeffe rearranged the single flower centerpieces, told patrons to look closely & pay attention if you want to get anywhere in this world, satisfaction a combination of generosity, delicacy, & patience. *Surrender to something greater than yourself,* she urged, & we all gaped in awe, the way only the profound can leave one apelike dumbstruck. Needing some fresh air, after making a brief argument that most things can, in fact, be black & white, Ansel Adams hit the road & just then Frank O'Hara burst in with his buddy Mike Goldberg who carried a bag of ORANGES, ordered SARDINES, & Frank whispered, *This would be so much better if everyone in here was gay & wanted to love me,* but he whispered it in a way that was clearly meant to be heard, if you know what I mean. Rothko again stacked his cheese blocks, Monet squinted, & Magritte— pissed about the lack of a *No Smoking* sign—hid behind his apple most of the evening. Frankenthaler gestured wildly at Hartigan, Basquiat over there spray painted his steak, & we didn't see him, but all of the sudden we noticed Banksy's self-portrait graffitied on the back wall. *Life's about two things*, said Man Ray, adjusting his camera pointed at sultriness in the corner booth, *First, it's all about editing yourself once you've opened yourself up to possibility, & second, & this is very, very important— Kiki, love, can you please be more, oh, je ne sais quoi, can you be more violin?— life is about* ▮ ▆ ▆ ▆ ▆ ▆ ▆

Promise Adventure

Growing up in the 70s & 80s
I thought I'd have to grapple
with the Bermuda Triangle
a lot more than I have, & the one
time I was actually in Bermuda,
they didn't even try to capitalize
on their global position, like
with tourist kiosks, t-shirts,
kitschy shot glasses & magnets,
& I haven't even mentioned
the ubiquitous & ominous
warnings for lava, space lasers,
twilight zones, jungle quicksand,
the rise of the machines—oh wait—
snakes amid archaeological ruins,
total thermonuclear annihilation,
or reversion to swordplay, whips,
little enchanted empathetic bears,
magical amulets, romance amid
international adventure or heck
even Amelia Earhart on an island
in the South Pacific, with her
flight jacket & aw shucks wave
& *Howyadoing* & *Whereyabeen?*
Just once I want theme music
to rise to a crescendo during
one of my classes, so I have to
grab my passports—yes multiple—
leather coat & fedora & rush off
to the waiting dodgy biplane
to save the world in a way
it didn't yet know it needed.

Bomb City

For my golden eighth birthday J
ohn Lennon got murdered
& I got a new *Star Wars* toy.
Ted Koppel's hair/soul less
comforting than *Mom's, Back up
there—don't make me tell you again*
as she fork-into-box ate leftover
cake & baby-bottle-fought
with my toddler sister
& I just wanted to know
things'd be alright. This was
just a handful of years after
CLE became nationally known
for union-built Fords exploding
in parking lots, & then the mob
finally got Danny Greene.
Kaboom. Even Rodin's *Thinker*
over on the cultured side of town
got nicked in one blast, & maybe
I'm conflating protest bombs, but
he's still there, contemplating
sulfur, scars, & the Wade Oval
Lagoon. You know, people who
possess power don't usually
give it up without a fight/blood
or the enormous passage of time,
& stained public concrete is
the worst case. And people
desperately spurned are more
likely to explode than go in
for another attempted hug.
Decency is we still haven't.

Situation: There's a Pint of Ben & Jerry's in Your Freezer. How Many Nights Does It Last?

Richard Dawson survey says the number
one answer is… zero. It's gone the night you
bought it, right? As it was a reward for another
hard week, & when the week started you said,
This week will finally be easier, right? *We're due
for an easy week, finally?* Or maybe you got
a smaller than expected raise, but it's still
something, or you didn't cry as hard as you
thought you would & being a human being
is often really hard, so Brownie Batter Core,
the entire pint filled with chunks of satisfaction
& only flecks of regret. Or you throw yourself
a small party in your head or you make yourself
a birthday cake & impromptu invite friends
& family to sing to you because during that
song is when absolutely everyone stops what
they are doing & is just present in the moment
focused on one thing, not on the globe spinning,
not on breathing or trying to circulate all
that blood or remember all the lessons you
were ever taught, & because there are few
spectacles that cause absolutely everyone to
stop & focus all at the same time, you bring
out the papery vibrant spectacle that is a
piñata & you & everyone hold their breath
as the one you love the most wipes her hands,
tightens her grip, secures her stance, & then
winds up for her hardest-ever swing, & you
& everyone anticipate the crack, can almost
already feel the candy falling, raining down,
bouncing like raindrops off your hands, off
the pavement, simultaneously wetting the
ground, fulfilling the desire, & exploding up,
cascading back up, the very fine mist painting
a brief & fleeting rainbow across the sky.

III.

Global Flavor Riot

Before you again ask me, *What would you like for dinner?* let me remind you that I became the default cook for my family A.) because of my wife's hectic work schedule & my lots-of-grading-at-home teaching schedule, & B.) despite the fact that I was raised on sawdust meatloaf & bland green beans I'd hide in mashed potatoes. And unflavored chicken strips, French Fries with no ketchup— never ketchup— & the fact that my mother-in-law would start the Sunday pot roast on Tuesday, cook all the juice & flavor out of it so it resembled a finely handcrafted Venetian leather loafer, then provide enough gravy to drown a veritable barnyard of swine, & somehow I'm the bad guy for pointing out that so much au jus might not be necessary if the Sunday roast was actually cooked, you know, on Sunday. My survival hasn't always been guaranteed. My cooking talent not something I could rightfully claim as a talent. Somehow, we've all become more assemblers than chefs, but somehow wife & I almost have almost raised three fine young empowered women who for the most part have barely never died as a result of our terrible palates. Dad jokes & mom's purposeful embarrassments, sure, but definitely not from processed foods reprocessed in our kitchen. Culture erupts when we move from the struggle for survival to the time & patience that an aesthetically pleasing dish might afford. And we've settled our family on the uncultured side of town. You understand that multiple truths can be possible at once, right? As in the Age of Discovery was the age of black peppercorns & Sri Lankan cinnamon sticks & cloves & mace & nutmegs. As in the Age of Discovery

was the age of remapping the map. The Age
of Discovery was the age of the church with
its black-&-cross-clad Jesuits stored next to
the limes & sauerkraut & hardtack biscuits
in the hold & was thus the age of sanctioning
domination, enslavement, genocide in the
name of Christ, bullies to the lesser people
it claimed to protect. Hey smalltown girl
living in a lonely world, you understand
you don't need to listen to Journey or Rome
& you can, in fact, stop believing anytime you
want? You understand the Age of Discovery
started the age of exotic feathers, textiles,
& homespun misogyny & cane to molasses
to rum to the terribleness of the Middle
Passage. We're all food for worms, but need
we be chattel, too? Such a thin line between
appropriation & allyship, bolder barrier
between reverence & revolt. Before
refrigeration replaced ice boxes replaced
ice blocks replaced root cellars, the three
ways to preserve meats were salting,
drying, & aciding, as in storing cucumbers
in vinegar vats. Smoking the forgotten
stepsister. Fat the absent father providing
initial energy then converted to resentments.
There's no accounting for bad taste. But like
most wise decisions, we'll only take credit
for our good tastes. The difference between
flavor & taste is that without smell, you can't
tell flavor, & we can't taste everything, &
we can't just go around licking everything
especially if our nose is plugged. Plugged
noses won't distinguish an apple chunk
from an onion. And yet flavor drives
consumption & the self-checkout lines.
Evolutionarily, due to daily diet shifts
over millennia, cats can no longer taste
sweets, pandas can no longer taste proteins,
& the GOP: women's rights, suffrage, nor
common sense gun laws. Because of high

content bitter receptors. My bitter receptors
are reserved for broccoli & those who spend
careers diminishing other's human rights.
So it's not that I'm a picky eater so much
as just born this way, with receptors &
neurons that don't taste the way you might
taste. You see, usually we don't seek flavor
silence, nor do we seek a flavor death metal
concert, preferring sweet & sour, lemon-lime,
& SweeTarts. Taste is only one ingredient
in the flavor equation. The difference
between flavor & taste is that you can
taste flavor, but you can't flavor tastes,
except in the circumstances where you try to
drizzle chocolate on a bad decision after it's
already been decided, a cascade of excuses
disguised as reasons, our species' inability
to take responsibility for taste's stink, so
we turn everything into a partisan spin
room. *No judgment or I'm not a racist,
buuuuuuuuuuuuuut…* the first red flags
in a litany of flags, a regatta of bad ideas
not disguised with sprinkles or coconut
shavings. And you're right Gwen Stefani,
This shit is bananas. B. A. N. A. N. A. S.
The truism of flavor profiles, as when
individual flavors combine & change
each other, which goes double for words
in the same sentence combining to form
not individuality but a larger collective
meaning beyond themselves, again with
the lemon-lime, or deep down, you're
really shallow, aren't you? So, what are
your high-definition flavors? Those that
make you sit up & take notice & maybe
you gotta get a photo of this dish for
your Instagram? The royalty of pineapple?
Or the dexterity of the potato, brought from
Peru to Louis 14's court, across the Channel
& eventually to the Emerald Isle? You know,
Sherman's march across the South was

as much about scorched earth as it was
about controlling the food supply, barns,
storehouses, railways, & Rebel economy.
And when Mao tried to mimic collectivization,
as Stalin did in Ukraine, the Chairman really
outdid himself, genociding at least 30 million
Chinese, poor rice & wheat farmers & women
& children & fodder for propaganda, whereas
Joseph air-quotes-only took out 7 million,
& selective history is still trying to rinse that
out of our mouths & textbooks, as if we govern
the state of Texas. The only one who has
any right to walk with arrogant swagger
is unapologetic, mother-F-ing nitrogen,
for once ammonia was lab-synthesized
by a German chemist in 1909, the globe
saw the biggest revolution the globe's
ever seen. And the Green Revolution
is still ongoing. And like Flavor Flav,
the giant clock is still ticking. Take this
à la carte tidbit: 20th century population
leapt from 1.5 billion to 6 billion all because
Bavarian lab nerd reproduced ammonia
from elemental nitrogen & hydrogen which
produced factory fertilizer & combined with
massive seed production, which produced
crops to feed us all many times over, except
those still-victims of hoarding stranded
on the outreaches, in the food deserts,
but then MTV's LIVE AID thought they
could fix anything. And gosh, I do love
Bono, & I admire him for trying, & despite
his cockiness, his arrogance can't compete
with institutional bureaucratic conceit.
When isn't hubris the major plot explainer
for our species? And so, nitrogen's the only
godly rock star, making up 78% of our air,
in every cell of us, & a primary driver of all
life forms. She'll surely tell us when we've
hit our food threshold, our population limit,
our mom admonishing, *Don't eat that in front*

*of everyone if you didn't bring enough to share
with everyone.* So, the Age of Discovery
was the age of epicurean development,
& Peter Piper picked a peck of pickled
peppers. My favorite cookies are no bake
chocolate oatmeal droppings dropped
on waxed paper & cookie sheeted into
the fridge. Here's that recipe you asked
for: ½ cup of premium Mayo County butter,
½ cup smooth milk from the creamiest cows
Hershey, PA has to offer, maybe a drop
of the extract from a Tahitian vanilla bean,
cocoa powder from the deepest Mexican forest,
two cups of pure sugar from the finest antique
cane in Papua New Guinea, & three cups
of Argentine oats. Don't under or over boil.
We're all just doing all we can not to boil
over, aren't we? In this way the recipe for
global commerce becomes the story of
gastronomic delight if we can stop thinking
about the barbarism. Dutch spice cakes—
gingerbread & mascarpone cheese—
the East India Company's answer to
objectional behavior was, *Here have more
cake.* Cake almost always makes everything
almost better. I blame the dinosaurs for
the skyrocketing gas prices: why couldn't
they go extinct more cheaply? The Age
of Discovery's descendants are Julia Childs
& Anthony Bourdain & Williams Sonoma,
& Crate & Barrel arose from Indonesian
cargo cults. We can turn any worldwide
phenomenon into a cult if we just believe
hard enough. And even Sinclair's *Jungle*
won't stop the dodgy factory owners
from not not doing the right thing; when left
to their own devices, when union busting,
because any oversight leaves a bad taste
in the mouth when you're trying to
operate out-of-sight. No accounting
for bad taste. The age of Marco Polo

was as much about making money & finding
fame as it was about finding spices or silk.
Before Britain was an empire of colonies,
it was an empire of the seas, an empire of
ships, sailing home foodstuffs from
around the globe to their shores, plots,
cottages, & kitchens. There's no accounting
for bad taste, & that's only part of why
Henry 8 wanted Newfoundland—so that
he could feed his expanding navies.
Which then helped fuel the Irish Potato
Famine with a million dead & a million
more fled for salt cod & currant. The roots
of progress interweave with repression.
Anemia, pellagra, & scurvy. Limeys.
And Shit on a Shingle as your go-to
appetizer for neighborhood potlucks.
Challah & ciabatta & Irish soda & early
colonists thought it was bread's divinity
that separated & segregated them from
the Indigenous peoples, bread into flesh,
water into wine, people into slaves, or
genocidal afterthoughts, the two original
sins of the country never penanced for.
Which is so bland & white bread of us.
The age of the Industrial Revolution was
about sugar. The Industrial Revolution
was about fabric. Agriculture. Ironworks.
Bread. Indentured servitude. Ironworkers
would consume 4 pounds of sugar per
week per half-pound of tea. The Industrial
Revolution was about trying to find
the proverbial garden of Eden or even
Kubla Kahn's pleasure dome, all while
destroying gardens, secret & otherwise,
nature, & all those lands that didn't belong
to you. You can take someone else's land
when you minimize the culture they've
stitched & sewn into their soil. Soil they
felt an obligation to, not exploitation of.
The spice network a rough draft for

the impending veins & arteries of global
oil & its ravages & how every single
aspect of modern life is so oil dependent,
& dependent, really, on dead dinosaurs,
so don't tell me you can't affect the globe,
global markets, & shipping lanes long
after you're dead. You want that power
65 million years after you're gone? I'd be
cool without that. In America, we run on
19 million barrels of liquid dead plankton
& dinosaurs per day. And long pig is
the cute nickname we've agreed upon
for the cannibalism of human flesh,
which tastes more like sweet lobster
than chicken. And the Boer War &
the Whiskey Rebellion. *Spices* derives
from *species* & Darwin is as important to
the future as he was to the past, as farmers
are to wealth. The privilege of the wealthy
is that they can impersonate the clothes of
& play working class any time they like,
as in *noblesse oblige*. Carrots weren't orange
until 16th century Dutch noblemen wanted
to impress their narcissistic orange king,
so they outbred the original purple & white
root vegetable into its sun-colored currency.
Do centuries of manipulating & hybridizing
foods mean that we aren't propagating food,
rather it's the food that is now propagating us?
Folks, we're talking about eco-evolutionary
gastronomy. The Mesopotamians & Inca
& Ancient Chinese independently sacrificed
to gods their veggies, animals, warriors,
& virgins, thinking that agri-sacrifice,
fertility given was fertility earned, as if
we're all living inside one interpretation
of Shirley Jackson's "Lottery?" *First thing
you know, we'd all be eating stewed chickweed
and acorns* & with just a little more sacrifice—
your son or mother or daughter—cosmic order
will be restored & the gods will again produce

food from their own mouths, & it never
dawned on them they possessed in their own
hands the power to close those godly jaws.
For my beloved & me, flavor nirvana
happened at a chic shabby restaurant
in Mykonos' harbor as we feasted on
chicken kabobs, rice, & saganaki with
a couple cool bottles of Retsina. Retsina
followed by the sweet salt kissed from
my wife's neck right there on the beach,
that goose fleshing spot right behind
her ear & onto her collarbone & this is me
yada-yadaing great sex. Have you ever
tried putting your peanut butter in her
chocolate or your chocolate in her peanut
butter? Watermelon sugar strawberry,
& me passing out on our honeymoon
after rum tasting for 45 minutes the first
time we landed in Jamaica. There's never
enough time for everything I want to eat.
Where's the elastic waistband when you
need it? We remember those memorable
meals so well because we're the future
products of past proto humans who needed
to remember what tasted good, because
if it tasted good, chances are it was nutritious
& we could ingest, digest, convert to cellular
energy, grow, evolve & look, presto-chango,
it worked. And now, with our abundance,
we can enjoy the *mmmm donuts* without
realizing that craving is unconsciously
a craving for certain nutritional nourishment
where calories & species development collide
on a nutrient-rich continuum. Which are
fancy words for: we're now more like
Pavlov's dog than we are Pavlov himself.
Cleveland to Constantinople to Venice
& Lisbon & Amsterdam as the capital
cities of the spice trade—they wouldn't
have gone out on the open seas if their food
already tasted good or there was enough of it

home-cooking. Treacle & Vegemite & Nutella
& peanut butter & anchovies & pickled
herring & onions & raisins & Brussels sprouts
& marsala & veal saltimbocca with prosciutto
& sage & al dente fettuccine. We built our cities
not at all on rock-n-roll, but instead we built
them in a manner as we would like to be seen.
Rather than how we really are. The remains
of St. Mark were smuggled out of Byzantium
& to Venice between prosciutto slices, so as
to hide them from the then customs agents,
get them to wharfs & hometown stevedores
& what a coincidence those relics landed
in the church that's in the square covered
in pigeons named after Mark himself. Sage
for a sage. One dedicated daughter replied
to her father that she loves him as much as
fresh meat loves salt. How would that simile
have changed if Willie Shakes had a fridge?
She'll never be mistaken as a Spice Girl,
Cordelia, stage name Cardamon Spice,
in her princess gown, the other two lyre
& luting along to *So tell me what you want,
what you really, really want / I wanna really,
really, really wanna zigazig ah*. Some of
the main differences between being classified
as a spice merchant or a pirate are: how strong
are you, how many weapons do you have,
& did you win a battle today? Only through
winning battles do we get to determine
what we call ourselves. Diet guides &
600-pound lives & let's talk about our
eating disorders. Pre-Columbian hunter-
gatherers had better diets than farmers.
Often, we don't realize the real damage
to ourselves we're doing until we've done
it. Bookmark secondhand tobacco & climate
change. Gradual shifts rather than instant
evolution. But still, instant karma's going
to get you, if you believe in that kinda thing,
amber fields of grain shining on, supplanting

one civilization for another, moon, stars,
& sun knocked right off their feet. *And
we all shine on / like the moon and the stars
and the sun /And we all shine on / On and on
and on, on and on.* Esoteric spices brought
from mystical lands. Ephemera & perishables.
Galenic medical theory—more metaphysical
than practical—suggested that anything
can be mapped according to its four points:
north, south, east, & west, connect to water,
fire, air, & earth, which connect to phlegm,
bile, blood, & black bile, which connect to
summer, fall, winter, & spring, the four
periods of mankind, the four periods of
the day, the four colors, the flavors, the four
evangelists, suits of cards, horsemen, & eyes.
But now we've discovered a fifth, so prepare
yourselves for a reading from the gospel
of umami, earthly & meaty mushrooms
a comfort in a season of mushroom clouds
& falling heavens. When science tries to do
nature better than nature: there are about
2,500 flavor ingredients in a real apple,
but only 25 in a sour apple Jolly Rancher,
& the Global Seed Vault in Svalbard, Norway
may save us all when we finally blow up
all but a few who start this greenhouse
all over again. Spices can correct our
ill tempers. Pharaohs were sometimes
buried with peppercorns in their nostrils.
Ever smell so bad that you can taste your
own stink? Sex, age, lifestyle, & climate
will explain your diet & pasty complexion.
Medieval doctors were called leeches
because of the blood they drained from
their humor-balancing patients. And waiter,
I'd like to speak to the manager about this
hodgepodge, jambalaya, polenta, curry,
Mexican Pizza, Toasted Cheddar Chalupa
Combo Meal, fish sauce, succotash, borscht,
goulash & gazpacho & gumbo & a smorgasbord

of cornucopias, a smattering of charcuterie,
siracha & guacamole & shepherd's pie,
bouillabaisse & mayonnaise & béchamel.
Garlic & cabbage & collard greens, ham
hocks & beetroot puree; haggis & coleslaw
& blackened peppered Iberian suckling pig.
Ceviche. Chickpeas & hummus & tabooli.
Orange juice pulp as if they are bits of
spiderwebs on your lips. Texture's everything
to taste. Margarine & I Can't Believe It's Not
& butter & lard & Crisco & pork fat & lamprey
pie & culture whores ripping off recipes
they didn't invent. Mario Batali & his
orange hair & oranger Crocs & Emeril
screaming BAM! to startle awake his late-night
Food Network audience. Sugar & spice
& everything nice. Flavor bugaboos &
peccadilloes & pet peeves, so that suddenly
we're eating all the movie theater popcorn
& drive-thru soda from the fountain more
out of habit than for their actual nutritional
value, which, when you really think about it,
it isn't all that different from most folks
still clinging to their original belief systems.
Reason & prudence no match for the body's
basic yearnings. Enough of this closeting,
cupboarding, & quarter-mastering.
Did you know that if properly consumed—
or maybe improperly consumed—nutmeg
has the power to produce a hallucinogenic
effect? Sure, I'll have another slice of French
Toast. Powder puffs from my lips as I
decline admitting to knowing where all
the nutmeg went. Yes, we are technically
all living through history. The question is,
will ours be recorded with the flavor notes
it deserves? There's a shop in Austin, TX
that makes Gasoline Rainbow ice cream
made with durian. It tastes the way petrol
smells: a blend of custard, hot socks, sauteed
onions, & a gas leak. Likely won't go

pop sensation like pumpkin spice. Warmth
a comfort as the cooler weather comes on.
Cinnamon & cloves heat you. Fact. Similar
to black, red, & green peppers—a burn, tingle,
& buzz. It's masochism light, not quite habanero
or Frank's Red or Tabasco or Louisiana Hot;
garlic & mustard & capsaicin & the colorful
Scoville heat scale & the Hungarian proverb
that *only the best paprika burns twice*, once going
in, once coming out. Wasabi & horseradish
& siracha & Szechuan & wing sauce & pain
is just another taste tape measure in a whole
toolbox of flavor tape measures. Repeated
exposure to capsaicin may reduce your pain,
allowing you to move up that table, but pain
isn't a competitive sport when we're in
the emotional arena. Hot flavor equals
benign masochism; personal emotional
trauma, not so much. Too much heat,
too much pain, blocks all flavor & your
tongue is left to tingle as if you just licked
a 9-volt battery. Many Amazonian birds
can't taste the capsaicin in their gobbled
chili pepper seeds, so unfettered by spice.
I mean, if you really believe birds are really
real, the heat to their beaks is only a mirage
to their mouths; they become active participants
in planetary seed distribution, birds the original
& ongoing & forgotten trading network,
Rand McNally never really able to draw
the invisible migratory avian contrail lines
in the sky, those feathered merchants soaring
just below our soap-bubble atmosphere.
No two species eat or die in the same way.
Miso & Saki & sour dough & bread & pretzels,
& sour apple Blow Pops & beer & hard cider.
Some populations invented sour beer before
agriculture was even thought of. It's all
about either killing or enabling bacteria,
right? The degree to which we're sour
aversive. If I'm being honest, being sour

aversive is sort of like living in Ohio in
wintertime. And if I'm being honest, Ohio
would be a lot less tolerable if we didn't have
all this beer. Fermentation. Which is nothing
more than the careful control of slow rot,
which again, isn't all that different from
voting blue in Ohio. Hell, at this point,
you ferment & microbe about anything
& us Buckeyes will drink it. Slop it up.
Swallow it. Even if it's like the myth of
Don't swallow your bubblegum because
it'll stay in your stomach for 7 years,
even after all the artificial raspberry
sweetener leaked out. Astringent & redolent
& sashimi & camphor & menthol & Wrigley's
spearmint breath mints & sure I'd love another
Black Seal Rum with ginger beer. Creamed corn
& smokey cigar & brown bread ice creams are
served in other locales. Vanilla bean with
caramelized brown bread crusts. Dunno if
those will catch on, but I'm very aware that
the lines between soda jerks & snake oil
salesmen, a doctor & a magician, have always
been tenuous. Turmeric might yet be a cure-
all for cancer. Pepper spray for protection
when walking back from the bar alone.
Pungent darkened alleyway. Manioc &
watercress & cassava. Millet & Johnnycakes
& flapjacks. Sorghum & soft maize. And
the Thanksgiving holiday was only begun
as a way to bring us all together post-Civil War,
but today, without due recognition of
the Wampanoag, those Massachusetts Bay
Companies still have their foots on throats.
A Mesoamerican recipe that breaks down
maize into nutrients that are easier to digest.
Like punctuation's job in well-written sentences
in a chaotic thought process. As in organisms
with teeth first developed teeth so that we
can eat things that are bigger than our
mouths & I've never been one to shoot

my mouth off, but when I do open it
I try to make sure I mean what I say.
The world changes. People don't. Menu
to buffet to banquet. Gathering to farm
to farmer's market, foraging to farming,
modified, domesticated, hybridized,
& propagated. And we still call them
gorilla sticks, not mozzarella sticks,
because of our middle child's word
aphasia she inherited from her mother
from her grandfather from her great-great-
great from her grand-Neanderthal doing
everything she can to communicate that
that appetizer might be a choking hazard,
so don't eat them while riding in an elevator
alone. Like blue corn, can't we all be
classified as genetic mutants? He who
controls food production & distribution
holds the ultimate power, a balance among
agriculture, industry, & warfare. Just ask
Napoleon & his failed siege in Russia.
Like cows, we're feeding machines,
& either you are fenced in or riding
the fence to make sure the barbed wire
is intact. Food is just history's invisible
fork. Gobble gobble. Like most interpersonal
interactions, the sense experience we expect
to have—sweet to salty—we actually do have,
which is why ice cream tastes better after
the home team wins instead of loses.
It's called sense integration. The flavors
exist in the molecules deep inside the mind
more than in the food itself. In other words,
thought itself is flavor itself. Which is why
it's impossible to think about raspberries
themselves, their plump summer sweet
juiciness, without actually picturing
raspberries themselves, their aggregate
drupelets candy to your brain. It's not
necessarily the volume of the ingredients
in the recipe that makes the meal. Rather,

it's the molecular weight, what's really there,
what can be measured on the microscopic level.
And when you think about it, that's really not
that different from human beings. Louder
doesn't mean actual substance. After all,
the process of cooking is applying carefully
measured heat to a set of carefully selected
ingredients pulled from the pantry shelves,
cupboards, from the fridge to the mixing bowl
to the oven, pulled from the oven, left to cool
on the counter for 5 minutes, & back to the
fridge in the leftover Tupperware. The goal
of cooking is to make those ingredients fall
apart & then recombine in a new & interesting
flavor. Sometimes, with the right amount of heat,
& just the right amount of pressure, we can take
even the simplest ingredients, like butter, sugar,
& cream, to make something really elegant
& flavorful, like caramel. Vanilla salted caramel.
Marzipan & baklava & flan & apple compote
& Malley's Milk Chocolate Covered Pretzels
& Girl Scouts' Thin Mints, Ben & Jerry's Chubby
Hubby & tiramisu & molten chocolate cake &
fried ice cream as an example of the cook's short-
handed, oversimplified diffusion equation is
L-squared equals 4DT, the distance traveled
by the diffusion front as a function of time.
Time always distancing, diffusing, &
denaturing us—atoms inside molecules
named amino acids, one thing always hiding
another thing, as Kenneth Koch points out,
because sometimes poets are easier to understand
than mathematicians are easier to understand
than physicists are easier to understand than
molecular gastronomists. Ever think how Eve
must've self-fertilized that first apple, those first
swallowed seeds into the first orchard, if you
believe in that kind of thing? Talk about diffusion
principles. And gosh, if that's not a metaphor
for what our existence is, I don't know what is.
So maybe we stop making celebrity chefs

out of every chef & making the best meal
out of every meal, & just enjoy each bite,
each dinnertime conversation. Because when
your picture making mechanism finally gets
crushed, you'll no longer get to savor those
peppercorns from Malabar, the cinnamon
of Zanzibar, the succulent shrimp plucked
from the blues of Adriatic water, the faint
yellow of Algerian couscous. The folly of
our haste flavored with merciless clearness.
So why don't we just light some candles,
clink our glasses & enjoy this still-hot meal?

IV.

When I Finally Began Talking to Myself In Sir David Attenborough's Voice

Because I've always been oversensitive to my own shortcomings, & if you think in British, immortality might arrive whilst wearing a many-pocketed travel jacket & worsted wool trousers amid artifacts inside perhaps a heavily tapestried natural history museum. Back when Earth's atmospheric oxygen content was 35%, common flies could boast a wingspan of 27"—a small television—or 10' centipedes could corkscrew down the forest floor, but now we're only at 21% oxygen, so the biggest an insect can get is 6½"—thank god, but is that still burn down the house territory for most of you? I must admit that that was 300 million years ago & who really knows where we'll be in another 300 million years, other than not here. Most of us think our mothers were here long before us, & in one sense you're right, thank you very much matrilineal DNA, but in another sense, you should have seen a mother's wingspan hundreds of millions of years ago. Let's just watch & see what she does next, what she decides to drag back to her burrow. What she leaves for the rest of the colony. And now I wonder if she's ever going to die, should-have-been-lethal-spinal-cord-injury & miracle surgery survivor & will it be, in yet another 300 million years, or 3 x 300 million, flying half robot & half microplastic filled giraffes with long beaks, extended warranty telephone salespeople, & Mom? Say, what exactly is the weather forecast for the next 1.5 billion years?

Wax Management

Your candle is lit even if you don't remember lighting it & it's the good one, the Fresh Balsam Single Wick from Bed Bath & Beyond or Bath & Body Works, you know there's a bath in there somewhere, a cleansing, but how the body works how the mind works has always confused you, & a Norwegian forest drifts through your house your living room, winds up the stairs the hardwoods & through the window on the landing you swear you can almost see through midnight to Scandinavia, through the ink to the Northern Lights, maybe only a trick of the mind, maybe alpine windchill, & as the guests arrive & the chatter rises, the flame still burns in its decorative almost mason jar over in the corner, slow releasing its scent, its worries, its anxieties & its depressions, & after a few drinks mixed with the new medication you're transitioning to, the booze becomes a toxin & almost like flinging your full Solo cup full of gasoline at the candle, & before you know it, the wall, the ceiling, the whole forest is on fire, mismanaged sparks into a conflagration into a party that ends in disaster in a self-harm attempt & you feel like you should have warned yourself & you vow to yourself your lover your family your doctors to keep the flame little & once again contained.

The Opposite of Anthropomorphic

Isn't having animal, bug, mineral, or vegetable characteristics, just as you'll never win the argument of tomatoes-as-fruit, even if you're right, even if everyone incorrectly associates them with Italy more than Mexico. The opposite of pineapple on pizza isn't pepperoni in your piña colada. The opposite of saying you're sorry isn't holding a grudge, & the opposite of a grudge isn't forgetting how much you were hurt. Time goes by just so fast, but there's a giant land tortoise who's outlived all 18th, 19th, & 20th Century monarchs. Maybe she knows something about metaphors, survival, & opposites.

The Age Where I Need to Take a Photo & Then Zoom In, In Order to Read the Fine Print

There's nothing more powerful than when someone else believes in you & that you'd, friend, purposefully withhold your belief in another in order to diminish that other, well that says everything about where you fall on the comic hero-villain continuum. Stan Lee wouldn't waste four colors on you. But just because you don't belong in this room, because it's become clear that no one else wants you in this room, & that you can't see that you're not wanted in this room, well that doesn't mean there's not a room for you. You're just not inside our entanglement theory. You're round, thick enough, you've a hole for an axel, & how on earth can that be enough? How can you roll without ever considering your wheelness? We're talking about niche construction theory, ecosystem engineering, response, & evolution. The problem with Zen Buddhist monks in a shopping mall is that they don't want stuff enough. They don't even rent or lease cars, let alone buy outright. They are the wheel cutting through the snow & you are the snowflake that never wants to feel responsible for the avalanche. A person's morality only has clear boundaries until there's enough cash on hand to permeate said boundary. Gosh, I want you to be a landscape that stands for values in a way that'd make John Muir proud.

Because The Weather Changes

Because I am about to be a father, I think everyone is going to be a father. Suddenly that woman & that woman & that woman are pregnant. An epiphany in line. The line for the bathroom because someone else said he had to go. And today everything, the leaves are crying, the sewers are crying, & I'm crying because cancer is raining in too many people. And I'm only concerned because I'm affected. Which could be shallow, but the dirt is never too far beneath the sheen. We always want, like kids near a pool, to splash if the others are. All those bouncy inner tubes. Cocoa butter & chlorine. Get me out of the sun. I'm sun-sick when I should be fluorescent & elastic. My wife is pregnant & here a relative is dying. I think unicycle & tomorrow unicycles on the sidewalk, unicycles on the bed, unicycles zipping open my head like bone saws. Exactly like bone saws.

Think About All the Things You're Not Thinking About

When you dig your toe into the hold in the batter's box, your extra pair of gloves back pocketed & you don't even feel them on your rump as you start to focus on the pitcher rubbing up the ball, trying to intimidate you from under his bill's low cap & you don't hear the crowd noise as it drops out as if your ears suddenly clog as if you're on a steeply ascending airplane & you don't smell the hotdogs or spilled Budweiser slowly cascading down among the peanut shells covering concrete as suds flow from the lower box seats toward the dugout toward the dirt that you can almost feel between your fingers; the dirt that's so fine but not powdery but almost soft chocolate microplastic beads & there's one stream of sweat carving across your forehead so you call for timeout so you can consider all the experiences you've been neglecting while you were focused on this one about to be brilliant moment.

I'm a Little Late to It, but Here's a Review of James Cameron's Humongous, Gigantic Blockbuster, *Avatar: the Way of Water* (2022)

Warning: Contains Spoilers.

Our young male protagonist struggles to find acceptance in a time & place where he'd like to be king of the world, but the socially stratified society that only thinly disguises the ravages of imperialism & misogyny stands in the way of his own self-importance. There's a lot of water. Some dancing. It gets loud. Sometimes enormously cinematic camerawork for the sake of being cinematic. Prudishness battles sexual liberation. Lovemaking is inferred. Lights, like magic, play tricks in the nighttime. Bioluminescence would be an unappreciated but still cool superpower. Handprints & majestic riches, wealth beyond comprehension, are tangled in the symbolism. In the climactic scene, a big ship sinks, & some passengers are literally handcuffed to the crumbling behemoth in an effort to heighten the tension. Duplicity ensnarls. Communication stalls. Children are props. *In loco parentis* isn't understood. Not everyone gets out. Permeable lines include the ones between championing the marginalized & refueling the powerful. Empathy versus contempt for. Eco-conservation versus shameless profiteering. We're told hearts will go on, but man's hubris likely won't allow it. Little's changed since the Greek Tragedies. Then again, as a species, we've only been writing words for 3,000 years. Again, it's a big movie. Almost as if it's obliviously compensating for something while trying to be subtle about being more than just a remake. What's not derivative but still worth seeing? There was room, Rose. There was room.

When Will You Stop Trying to Live Up to the Length of Your Own Shadow?

Time comes closest to stopping when your bare chest connects to their bare back, the comforter, in its hypoallergenic polyester silkiness, still carrying the coolness from the windows-open blue afternoon, & for now, it's evenly spread, yet slowly warming, & the skin's layered textbook diagram is colorful under a microscope: epidermis & swaying-like-a-wheat-field follicles almost snap click together, as if organic Legos. That air around that weld keeps warming, threatening more heat than most could bear & three choices present: slide back over, alone, to your vast ocean of mattress, or two, slip down the covers & let the ceiling fan do its goosepimple duty, or, lastly, to stay right there, allow the heat to simmer to boil to bake to broil like a field in the sun all the way to the horizon, which stays distant & just out of reach, even as you keep walking toward it.

A Self-Perpetuating Cycle of Self-Perpetuation

Billy Joel got at least one thing right about *when you wake up in the morning with your head on fire and your eyes too bloody to see and you go on and cry in your coffee & you wake up late for school, and man you don't want to go and you ask your mom please, but she still says no.* It's not that you want to steal their thoughts, so much as they're in your bedroom & murmuring—conversations are being had & you want to participate in, not co-opt those conversations, beastly cacophony, but you don't know how to break into those closed-off circles of friends & acquaintances as when the fenced-off circles of the Venn diagram no longer overlap but instead separate & move to the extreme reaches of the enormous room & so you search the vast & empty space between those tight circles & your social awkwardness has never helped anything. Exactly what kind of soirée is this supposed to be anyway, Boys? And so, when you wake up at night, you wake up anxious. When you're awake, seemingly more awake than you've ever been, you think about how walking outside barefoot often helps, but I live in Ohio & the weather's only part-time, just barely conducive, conductive as if I'm a generic grocery store version of Nikola Tesla, trying to gather Earth's electrical impulses to calm soothe his brain as part of his morning ritual. He was the first to receive & administer electrical stimulus as therapy, even if he was his own grocery store generic version of a psychotherapist, imagining in 1899 from Pike's Peak that in the future world most humans would have handheld wireless writing journals we'd charge by inserting, plugging into the earth almost anywhere & we could share our pages our thoughts on the tides of radio waves, ebb & flow, wirelessly, across the globe. But Tesla never lived in godforsaken Ohio, where walking around barefoot outside isn't always possible because of the weather because even daffodils have to wrestle April snow stiff winds again. Heads bowed, but not in self-reflection, admiration, or supplication, but in just-trying-to-make-it-through-top- heavy circadian rhythms or because it's 3am again & all the neighbors already think I'm weird & their care for me couldn't be less—or maybe it could be less, because we're always deluding ourselves about the bottom limit of how much we could care about anything & almost always misspeaking *could & couldn't.* When those Pikes Peak anxious moments arrive again at 3am, I picture my brain as a phosphorescent & glowing smartphone screen with all the pinging red bubble notifications on the corners of all my worry applications, & I try to slide them closed. Flick flick flick. They alert alert alert & why won't this bleeping thing smoothly slide off the bleeping screen, off the mind, like or as others seem capable of doing because they've all seemingly easily learned how not to care less—or not at all—& all I want to do is rest & wake up refreshed, ready to control the tides more than they—like a fast-moving tsunami—control me.

The Time I Brought a Vase Half-filled with Water to Bed

As I worked my way around your body, I used the tip of my index finger fingernail to slowly, carefully—as if delicately unpeeling the corner of a stubborn sticker from its backing—lift the edge of your calla lily tattoo from your ribs, the blooms giving slight fragrance to your back & perfect right breast. As the ink gradually began to unstick, the flowers blossomed from 2-to-3D, stalks filling my palm, & I placed them in the cobalt bedside vase. Next, a heavy-inked & vibrantly colored sunflower from your slightly vibrating thigh, the flower's large face slowly turning back toward the skin where it used to receive its light, its nutrients, its energy. And then the lotus flower from your sternum, a daisy from your toe, a ring of roses unlacing your ankle, & slow-spreading groundcover, in the form of a four-leaf clover, from just above the dimple on your rear end, & soon enough, I had a bouquet of you, from you, & for once even the morning birds fell silent, as your fragrance filled & drifted through our quiet home's open window screens & back out there, like a fine mist, replenishing nature.

V.

On Becoming My 75-Year-Old Mother's Medical Marijuana Plug

Maybe she suffered a spinal cord injury,
has glaucoma, ALS, Alzheimer's, cachexia,
cancer, chronic traumatic encephalopathy—
maybe she played line for the Steelers—
Crohn's, epilepsy or another seizure
disorder, fibromyalgia, hepatitis C,
Huntington's, inflammatory bowels,
MS, multiple diagnoses, pain that is
either chronic & severe or intractable—
when isn't pain chronic & severe or
intractable, emotional, emphatic,
or even sometimes never reaching
parasympathetic? My lack of telepathy
& her privacy settings making difficult
the multiple choice of apathy, empathy,
sympathy, or antipathy, so perhaps
a symphony of Parkinson's, HIV+,
sickle cell anemia, Spasticity or maybe
Tourette syndrome or a fall, a TBI,
or ulcerative colitis. Or maybe she's
been depressed for years, at least
since her hero-father-whose-care-she-
hospiced-herself passed in 2009. Or
maybe she has post-traumatic stress
disorder from something she's never
told us about, because telling your kids
everything about your life isn't part of
the job description, even if maybe
vulnerability would be a relief, but
even when you sacrifice part of your
life for the lives of others doesn't mean
others are all always entitled to more
sacrifice, answers, unearthing of secrets,
just as children always end up forever
shielding parts of their own lives from
even their very own mother, or a priest
in a mahogany ostentatious confessional,
god, the entire freaking universe. Maybe
she's got an eye toward becoming a 21st

Century trippy feminized Romantic poet
& plans on writing her own version of
"Kubla Kahn," her Xanadu pleasure dome
filled exactly with the exotics & Neil Diamond
timbrels she's so well-earned. Maybe even
she just adores *Dazed & Confused,* Cheetos—
Oooh-better-yet Andy Capp's Hot Fries
dipped in extra chocolatey milkshakes
with a Kit Kat & Snickers for dessert,
or maybe it's all about her love of Matthew
Alright-Alright-Alright McConaughey, Seth
Rogan, Snoop, Martha Freaking Stewart,
or that your kindly old neighbor you
never suspected would puff would
puff, & maybe maybe maybe maybe
maybe maybe maybe maybe, like most
healthcare decisions decidedly white
& old & *do-as-I-say-&-not-as-I-do*
male politicians make, it's none
of their goddamn business why.

Sometimes You Don't Know You're in a Bubble Until It Pops

There's a traveling rodeo out in Idaho
where one of the main spectacles
now includes clowns, cowhands,
& barely vetted audience volunteers
& they slip giant inflatable wearable
bubbles over their heads their shoulders
& no indemnity waivers just trust,
& the bubbles insulate them above
their crowns to just above their knees,
partially transparent scuffed plastic
& barely enough bulging eyesight,
as if too big myopic goldfish stuffed
into too small bowls & the goldfish tails-
turned-legs stick out the bottom—as if
some brightly colored Dr. Suess
illustration, primary colored & laced
with a morality tale—to run around
the ring looking for water for safety
for air because there's an underfed
& angry bull hard charging those
effervescent bubbles, like champagne,
sending them fast careening into
the gates the boards the dirt one another—
goddang, did you see her absolutely
go absolutely flying?—as if unattached,
unaware atoms aggressively trying
to outrun another, bounce off another
trauma, &/or maybe become part of
a molecule again. Bonding. Belonging.
The fear of not. It's hilarious & actually
a little twisted & dark when you really
stop to think about it: bulls & human
ping pong balls & inevitable suffering
on parade, an almost purposely
confusing & messy metaphorical
mashup & predestined spinal cord
injury or death & grief all in one,
& it's often much easier to simply
participate in the spectacle—to parse

words, hold tongues, or split infinitives—
than it is to walk away from its dangers,
which are, of course, more obvious to
the folks, the onlookers outside the bubble
than those in it. And yet, audiences
& legions of friends & family participate
perpetuate, not always willfully, but
also not as blindly as they'd first excuse
first have you believe & because
how can we not help but be dazzled
by the spectacle, as that's exactly
what spectacles are designed to do,
& oh did I mention that the bull
the entire ring the whole extravaganza
is just like living inside a large bowl
arena family filled with generational
alcoholism?

Terminal Uniqueness

> *The beginning is the most important part of the work. (Plato, The Republic.)*

Look, while therapy's been great for me,
has changed my perspective on—panoramic
shot of a *Christ the Redeemer* type of person
on a mountain, maybe vast desert behind
& a calm sea to the horizon, slow pullback
to pale blue dot amid swirling star clusters—
I understand it may not be great for you,
as you're unique, special, & simply there's
no therapist who would understand. I get
the *I'm glad it worked for you, but it wouldn't
work for me* because I once said *I'm glad
it worked for you, but it wouldn't work for me*,
before I allowed myself to realize I'm not
as special as you raised me to think. And
the excuse of somehow being restricted by
your status in the Boomer Generation, so
you just can't or won't or don't have to deal
with your shit, well not in that way, honestly,
is shit. The biggest explainer of why things
go so terribly wrong for protagonists in
movies/novels comes from the Greeks,
who once also thought themselves the center
of the universe: hubris. Excessive pride.
What's cool is that Socrates taught a thing
or two or three to Plato, who then spread
the good word, & eventually taught Aristotle,
who eventually mentored Alexander the Great,
who then built that great library, a repository
of memories, because as great as he was,
he also realized he/it/they wouldn't last,
& sometimes in order for ideas to last
beyond this terminal condition, we need
to speak, chisel it into clay, cry a little,
surprise yourself by how much you cry—
Jesus, why can't I stop crying?—be
vulnerable enough to turn yourself

from a statue back into someone willing
to be a real dumbass, much like the rest
of us, & if you don't, then the cost is—
well the cost should be entirely clear
to you to me to us by now.

Anxiety Mascot

Given my prowess at recreational
anxiety, I'm thinking of starting
an anxiety club team, eventually
accumulating enough points to earn
promotion to a semi-pro division,
& eventually fanatics & hooligans
will be obsessed with wearing
our kits, brand-name cereal
sponsor emblazoned across
the chests & choosing our players
first for their upcoming season's
fantasy league draft. Our riddled
squad will spawn blogs & websites
& Twitter accounts & parody Twitter
accounts, maybe even someday,
like the Savannah Bananas,
we'll be ridicule-slash-honored
on SNL, if/when it gets good again.
The fact is most of us hope
to pass on only our good traits
to our kids. My three have yet to
thank me for their combustible-
rocket-fuel anxieties. As when
the house no longer whispers
There must be more money & has
moved on to 3am comet trails of
*I finally have the perfect comeback
& I wonder if that kid from 6th grade
is still mad at me & what about this,
what about this, & what about this?*
The quickest path to human-slash-
wild-animal conflict is A-to-B-
straight-up feeding wild animals,
either purposefully or accidentally,
as in not securing rubbish containers
or leaving food offerings at shrines
outside the village & soon normally
human-shy animals will take
a risk to get more of that food,

gradually moving toward
the town's center as offerings
subside, so the wild animals
stalk in toward the townspeople's
doorsteps as shyness becomes
trained comfort & comfort becomes
trained fearlessness & fearlessness
unleashes natural aggression &
aggression means people die.
*They're GRRRREAT! a slogan
for both cartoon tigers & real &
now well-fed tigers.* As with
wild animals, with wild anxiety,
the line between adorable &
deplorable changes based on
what side of the barbed wire
barrier you're on, & to suggest
that *We're all a tad bit zooey a
nyway, so let's get Prozac in
the water supply…* well that
undermines the fact that many
are for-real fighting like hell
to free their one foot that's
already caught in the trap.

It's Magic, When Folks Don't See the Science Behind It

The used-new-to-me car
has this wizard feature
wherein the cruise control
automatically matches
the speed of the vehicle
in front of me, slowing
down or speeding up
accordingly, & if I begin
to drift from my lane,
it beeps, autocorrects,
& centers me, back inside
my glowing & pixelated
Frogger box-cage-you-
are-here-&-safe-blue-dot,
but as I commuted this
morning, the future-is-now
feature beeped-switched off;
not because of torrential rain
or blinding-white-out snow
as previously, but because
its buggy eyes couldn't quite
see ahead because the sunrise
high-hurdling over the horizon
straight ahead was enormous
& brighter than it's ever been
& the dang-new technology
for once couldn't quite keep
pace with the wonder.

Everyone is Walking Along—Floating Along—& You're the One with a Stone in Your Shoe

My kid brother dropped off his
10-year-old daughter so he could go
to therapy, & of course by kid I mean
3 years younger, one of us 50, one of us
pushing it. One of us constantly seeing
math word problems where none is
meant to exist, & the other expressing
anxiety/depression through other
peccadillos. We rode about 3 miles,
my niece & I. She reminded me
of when my daughters still lived
at home & were impressed with
small things Dad could do, pulling
a quarter from their ear, magically
changing the minivan's radio station
with an *abracadabra* flick of the fingers
when they didn't yet realize Chrysler
had introduced steering wheel
buttons. We're always not seeing
stuff when it's right in front of us,
aren't we? But how others perceive
us isn't supposed to be our problem,
right? So much time spent looking
back or forward. I mean, the moon
was rising on a shorts & shirtsleeves
summer evening as Lanie & I bicycle
bumped over uneven sidewalks,
the remnants of the busy corner
shoppe's orange swirl sugar cones
on our lips our chins our just made
memories.

Sofia the Flying Telescope

You don't need a spyglass to see back
into your own history, into what might've
been, never was, or where exactly you
made the correct choice—thin line between
reflection & regret—insight, foresight,
& potential. How a glass & a mirror
can shift from one to the other & back
with even the slightest of head tilts
isn't all that different from the thin line
between envy & empathy. You know
the last photograph Dad ever took
of his mom came after his father cracked
him across the jaw, ordered him up
to the funeral home to get a pre-wake
Polaroid of his dressed-in-white-but-gone-
before-fifty Mom. The makeup didn't
do a great job of masking the liver
cancer's yellow skin side effect. How
often our masks are more transparent
than we first assessed. Something less
personal here means the still surface
of a puddle-filled pothole. Beauty in decay
life's continuance, the forest floor's
humus, & humans rarely get to see
the atmosphere's thin line & even if
we did, we need boundaries on our
empathy, slowly built immunity to the
breaking news reports, because
we'll never accomplish anything if
we're constantly reminded of how
quickly it can all go away. Microscope
into kaleidoscope. That photograph
that Dad snapped? It was the sole
photo of Grandma Jeanne that
Grandpa Fred kept on his bureau
the rest of his life. Not their wedding
photo. Not a family portrait. Not 9
kids in Sunday's best on the Nicholson
& Lake front porch. It sat there, that

overexposed death mask, propped
against his cherry watch box next to
the dusty but cherished July 25, 1969,
Time Magazine featuring Neil Armstrong,
the final grand world event Grandma
Jeanne would ever witness. Thin line
between observable & infrared light
25 million light years from Earth's
curve, as if glimpsed from the high
speed high flying open door of a 747
because if we can see back far enough,
we might understand what comes next.

Ignorance of the Present

Harry Truman never wanted to be
President, but rose from the muddy
water, the town of big canoes, insisted
on pronouncing his home state with
an end A instead of its on-paper I—
Missouri Missoura Missouri Missoura—
& went on to serve two terms,
drop a bomb or two & said that,
really mindbogglingly, wasn't even
the toughest decision of his presidency,
see Korean War or Israel's creation,
& none of us can undo what's already
been done. You can't stop it, despite
all these desperate attempts. You're
coming of age unlike David Copperfield,
whether you like it or not, & you can't
go back, can't backspace, can't turn
this sandstone back into sand, these
berries back into a bush. There's been
a dead doe at the side of the road
all summer now, & she's started
to look like a deflated balloon
version of herself rather than
herself. Her insides inspiring life
in too many insects to count, because
as soon as you start pinning all
of them to the black felt of your
display case, they can't help but
inspire more.

Burning Birds & Fiery Jets: Mayday Mayday Mayday is French for Help Me

Late night, when Bridget's already
been in bed for hours, & that last glass
of wine has me a bit wobbly, or sentimental,
or both, I enjoy earbud-watching short v
ideos on my phone—those soundplugs
because-or-as-if it's something to be a
shamed of, as almost everything was
made to be, as I was raised in an ecosystem
of omnipotent, omnipresent, someone's-
always-listening-watching Old Testament
sort of crippling trifecta of spirituality:
not father, son, & holy ghost, but
humiliation, shame, & holy-living-hell
guilt. But now the videos I prefer aren't
porn or soldiers reuniting with their dogs
at airports or with kids at school assemblies
as some sad Sarah McLaughlin song,
the only kind of Sarah McLaughlin song,
overlays the action. Why's the whole
goddamn school gotta witness a soldier
mom hugging her gawky awkward
middle schooler who's already had
his share of beatings at the hands of
the football team? No. Not me. I prefer
to get weepy eyed at those golden
buzzer moments. You know the ones
from the reality TV loud talent shows
where a petrified contestant overcomes
her stage fright, her having-to-recount-
bullet-point her whole life's trauma to
the-audience-backed-4-judge panel—
a bit sadistic if you ask me—before
performing the most important audition
of her life & then with her first notes
she quickly turns the audience from
petty critics to awed cheerleaders &
absolutely nails the song & the confetti-
rains-down-on-her better than it did

all those times in her head, better than
all those times when her inspiration for
taking this leap—her mom or grandfather
or lover or child—was still with her, alive
& cheering & the trauma hadn't yet
been fully realized. People are actually
quite terrified of choice. Because once
given freedom to choose, people
are petrified they're going to make
the wrong choice & then be held
responsible for the ensuing carnival
of such choice & in that paralyzing way—
even if we're not all Hamlet-paralyzed—
accountability terrifies people far more
than choice. And the birds will do what
birds do, invisible migration routes
mapped into the sky blue above,
between & through the clouds.
When hasn't the privilege of travel
been a requirement for more food,
sex, or living a good life instead of
merely existing? Nature's always been
the template for a fighter jet's wings,
& yet there are only 66 years between
that first flight among all the squawking
gulls on a Carolina beach & Neil & Buzz
walking on the birdless & silent beach
of the moon. Amazing what we can
accomplish when we work together.
Governments & people trade in secrets.
Birds don't. Even if they know something
about existence that they haven't formed
the words for yet. And anyway, we only
like secrets when we get to be the one
to hold them & then decide when & how
to release them. Parakeets or controversial
opinions. It's not that we shouldn't ever
talk about politics, sex, or religion in polite
company, but that we've never been taught
how to respectfully have those difficult
conversations without fists, guns,

or crusades. And now that we're adults,
too many of us feel like we're finished
learning, so the only thing more carved
in stone than our righteous indignation
is our stubborn insistence that we're
as learned as we ever need to be. *Did you
know that smiling politely burns the same
amount of calories as speaking your mind?*
Most people tell you to just get over it.
Just get over your trauma or anxiety or
illness, as if you've never thought of that.
As if you can't not think/hope for that
eventuality. But time always passes too
fast when we want it slow & too slow
when we want it fast. Which isn't
too different from the act of mating,
dining, or nesting. With that face you're
now making at me, it's as if you're trying
to claim the right to be unhappy. To be
unhappy, to grow old & impotent &
insolent & get syphilis or worse or be
tortured by unspeakable things or
cancer or death & you won't even
manage a knowing & wry British smile
like Aldous Huxley. Bro, your world
ain't brave if you've never once questioned
everything you've ever learned. When
did suffering become a competition?
A card game with an ace in the sleeve?
As if you have a right to be savage
again, as if you have the right to eat
architecture; eat archeology & biology
& chemistry & physics & all the elements
that make us, us? As if you've the right
to listen to the wrong kinds of music
& think the condiments you love are
the best & only condiments ever
invented, but then it turns out that
salad is just mostly crunchy water
& ketchup is mostly tainted sugar
which means in a way it's not all

that different from Caribbean rum,
spiced or not, the spice never hiding
the fact of colonization's role. The fact is
if we want to get really good at something
we have to live a life with our obsessions
without letting those very obsessions
dominate or injure every other aspect
of life: family, friends, or work, as if we're
constantly juggling Venn diagram circles
way above our heads—airborne ikigai—
way up above like flaming knives or
chainsaws, & while those burning circles
might eclipse in front or behind each other,
moon hiding sun hiding planets or vice-versa,
partial eclipses are preferable to clanking
& crashing & open & about to be bloodied
palms upturned toward the implements,
birds, & spiraling galaxies beyond. You
are not Vlad the Impaler, nor should you
want to be. Don't seek suffering. Like bird
droppings on a newly waxed car, suffering
just has an opportune way of finding us.
M'aidez m'aidez m'aidez. Unlike jets landing
on an aircraft carrier, a steaming postage
stamp amid the emptiness of an otherwise
empty sea, most birds can't complete
migration as if marathoners, crossing
the finish line exhausted, dehydrated,
collapsing into the arms of a first aid
worker. Birds need to arrive, build
a nest, find food, mate & raise young
& make the most of the seasons before
the wind & snow & ice kick up again.
Unlike the old people & the ducks, us left
here in Ohio in January think we're too
smart to follow migration's roadmap
to Florida. The fact is, we all can't be
a Wallace Stevens poem. Suit & knotted
tie to sell insurance, but a poetic-freak
in the sheets. *Let be be the finale of seem.*
But really folks, it's just once again

stubbornness superseding fact-based
knowledge. *Tour de force* translates as
feat of strength, but more often than not,
strength's nobility resides in withholding
rather than using force. And so again I ask,
what are you going to do when someone
steps up to the cliff's edge? Are you going
to edge up to the edge of your seat & greedily
rub your hands at their potential catastrophe?
Or are you going to root for an earned,
if surprising success? Will you revel
in the majesty of their unfurled wings?

The Archeology of the Ampersand

Question: how often do you battle
the instinct to hate the group project—
with one unfair grade for everyone
in it—& yet desperately need to get,
to be, to remain connected to others?
The conflict of belonging but belonging
on your own terms. Boundaries
impersonating amoebas. It turns out
that on those job skills profile & value
assessment personality tests, I'm a
0% match for military service, & I've
only been tossed in the back of two
cop cars, once for questioning
the officer's color spectrum perception
as we both gazed up at the traffic light
& once for correcting the dude's grammar.
Listen, buddy, if you're going to hold
me to the bullshit stop at a stop sign
for 3 full seconds law, well then *Dreyer's
English: An Utterly Correct Guide to Clarity
and Style* would like a word. Note: if
you're going to correct a cranky cop's
pronouns, do so with the flair that only
middle aged white dudes assured of
their personal safety can muster. And
definitely don't slam your hand on
the back seat's plexiglass to correct
him again as he radios-in your
pomposity. Don't ask him about real
crime, broken windows theories,
or the criminal ways we're treating
the Earth, wild fires raging, plastics
& Prozac in our drinking water, &
Hey, you got any water up there?
you say to the sky or to no one in
particular, as he pulls you from
the cruiser, releasing you into your
own custody, when all you really
wanted to know was if he felt

the same, constant & persistent
& anxious push & pull—are we
all really that connected & can I even
be connected to those first century
Romans, whether through handcuffs
or hieroglyphs?

VI.

There's Documented Evidence of Telegraph Operators in the Distant & Almost Completely Isolated Operation Stations of the American Southwest Falling in Love, Despite the Century Beginning With 18, the Tumbleweeds, the Single Iron Wire, Poles Impersonating Cacti, Dots, Dashes, Omissions, Hesitations, False Starts, & At-First-Unobvious-Yet-Still-Horrific Anti-Indigenous Propaganda

So don't tell me your love
is somehow lesser than
just because you used
an App, even if her photo
was a beta version of herself
& technology is still mostly
understood as magic until
it's really understood via
experience, as when one
woman wanted to impress a
traveling fella & thus tried
to pour her famous homemade
thick tomato soup down the
telegraph line. Electrocution
isn't never a laughing matter,
especially for distant writers.
When are you going to
shift from survival mode
to living mode? There are
only 37.5 billion acres of
land on the planet & no
one other than the Dutch
& the random South Pacific
volcano are making more,
& not even enough to keep
pace with the ice melting
in your fizzy glass of Coke
& a smile, so what are you
going to do with your
mortgaged .3 acres? Build
more fences in a desperate
attempt to avoid the idea
that you're just a placeholder?
Exclusion often comes down

to which side of the fence
you're on, & savagery gets
defined differently depending
on if you're the conquered
or the conqueror. Barbed
wire's invention led directly
to Americans having heart
attacks in droves, as once
you fence in cattle, you can
contain, hyperbreed, & soon,
at least compared to evolution,
Mmmm bacon cheeseburgers.
I fell in love when I was
least expecting it, her breath,
perfume, & pheromones
the only technology on
the wind, & when you full
stop & think about it, owning
earth is as ridiculous as
owning air, another, or
magic itself, so are you
going to continue to focus
on possession, or for once
finally admit, given the
documented percentages
& actuarial tables, for once
finally realize that if we
really wanted to be sticklers
about it, we'd call Earth
Water?

Well, Well, Well… As If It Isn't the Consequences of Our Own Actions

The toughest thing about coaching
soccer for ten-twelve years wasn't
the players, but was the parents:
neck veins bulging, dramatizing
every breath, step, pass, mistake
little Sarah made, often wildly air
diagramming to her how to unstitch
the seam between the inattentive
fullbacks, as if these misty cool
Saturday morning fans—dew-covered
shoes & shouted breath like dragon
smoke—were all Pep Guardiola
understudies, yet too busy in their
own very important professional lives
to take the visor, clipboard, whistle.
And while I always appreciated it,
maybe I didn't appreciate it quite
enough, when during a U-8 fevered
pitch coed rec league match,
Charlie, one worthy atom in an
infinite universe, a future middle
& high school brutal bullying
victim, just stopped-plopped-sat
down on the field in the attacking
third because a delicate monarch
butterfly alighted on his forearm,
& sill today I never get tired of
seeing-remembering when absolute
& absolutely fleeting wonder… strikes.

I Always Thought That Elton John Song Went, "Hold Me Closer, Tony Danza"

Which is just one of the things
I was completely wrong about,
but as I've aged, my comfort with
misunderstanding has grown,
like an ever-expanding abstract
expressionist painting in a drafty
barn, no longer saying, *I understand
what you're doing there,* while
pointing, squinting, tilting my
head as if some prim critic or
confused dog. Another thing I
don't understand is my wife's desire
for a dog, as Bridget so seldom
has down time that it'd be no
more than 45 minutes of evening
cuddling with said dog before she
dozed off, TV light discothèquing
the bedroom, & me, after an hour
in the living room bookmarking
APL sites, learning that German
Shepherds were only invented
a few years before World War I,
16 million animals stitched into
part of that map of the dead,
those cuddlers just as confused
by the trenches, the whoosh
of the warfare on the wind,
or maybe the gentle lavender
breezes of French fields blowing
across our faces here in Ohio as
we consider how we usually
refuse to adapt ourselves,
& how we might still.

Like Frogs Around a Pond

In your leaps from lily pad to
lily pad, have you learned how
to control the chaos of your life?
Lilly pad from the struggle for
daily individual survival, a diet
of flies & long-legged water spiders
to lily pad society, hunter/gatherers
to lily pad farmers to lily pad sailors,
to social heritage spread like a lily
pad blight virus fungus, epi-to-pandemic,
to distant lilypad lands all around
the rim of the Mediterranean to society
to a lilypad of checks & balances of
baser lilypad instincts, morality like
a sunrise blooming from religion or
even only a library, lilypad civilization
sprouting cattail culture, one magenta
lotus against a purple-blue backdrop,
those things that make humans more
human, literature & theater, a mixed
tape or playlist, makeup & perfume
& are these glitter leggings too much
for me? Doesn't the way the light
catches the glint make my incredible
calves look even more fabulous? No,
you can't sleep with me or dip me in
garlic butter & only take a nibble,
my matrilineal DNA setting a clearer
boundary than my desire to be loved.
Cherished. Remembered. Competition
in constant strain against cooperation.
As long as there is poverty, there will be
religion, & as long as I'm wealthy with
culture, I'll never be poor.

How to Cultivate Political Propaganda

Many of nature's coolest plants have
a built-in defense mechanism to keep
that plant from being *completely* eaten
by predators dressed up as wandering
herbivores—just take, for instance,
the not-humble-anymore *Coffea arabica*
specimen, whether cut from native Ethiopia,
ancient Persia, stolen clippings for another
greedy European monarch, or even the
now-high-peaked & cool-morninged
Guatemalan climes. This gorgeous little
plant with her glossy green leaves & small
white flowers & bright red cherries—
each fruit containing two small bean pods,
slowly roasted from green to brown-black—
is presumably delicious exactly because of
her colorfully loud eye-catching spectacle,
but those bitter beans, without yet the
temperance of a soy milk or Splenda,
might just be too bitter for complete
consumption. Put another, clearer way:
a hungry animal can only tolerate
a coffee bean or two, not the *entire* plant,
& once that snack is chewed is drunk is
devoured, the snacking animal gets that
caffeine jolt we all crave, but to the animal it's
like a two-shots & unpleasant beer buzz,
an uncomfortable little toxin trip, perhaps
passing out next to the caterpillar &
too stoned Alice. Importantly, the caffeine-
the-toxin isn't enough to kill the consumer.
Because again, like most plants with a similar
defense mechanism, if the mechanism actually
killed instead of befuddled, nature, evolution,
the hybridization of unnatural selection,
would breed out the marauders susceptible
to death, making their stomachs, brains,
nervous systems more tolerant of the poison,
& in just a matter of time, born would be

venom-resistant predators & entire plants
gardens plantations would be wiped out
by the death-impervious-super consumers.
So again, the key is to breed your plant
with just-the-right-amount-but-not-overdose
amount of dizzy-drunk toxins. And voila,
microdosing. This is to say: in those small
doses, thanks to the birds & trade winds
in charge of initial seed migration, your
coffee your ideas might more easily spread
continent to continent, isolated atoll to
isolated atoll, idealogue to outraged
idealogue, voter to jacked-up-on-espresso
voter, & soon enough it's almost impossible
to distinguish predator from prey.

How Often We Store Our Memories Outside Our Minds

For Danny

User manuals in a jumbled mess in
a milkcrate in the front hall coat closet,
grocery lists on index cards, the cardboard
box with the recipe directions plucked
again from the rubbish because how much
of what did it say you next add to the
sauté pan? A hasty ballpoint scribble
in the fleshy webbing between your
thumb & index finger when no vellum,
parchment, or papyrus is near—
no papery wasp nest as the inspiration
for transforming all of civilization.
Clay pot inside clay pot, containers in
container, photograph of photographs,
why inside why, & ideas of the past
confused with ideas of the present,
so much so that the water jug doesn't
not produce because it's empty, but
instead because it's so muddled, unsure
of which molecules to release first. As in,
we now know more about the Romans than
even the most learned of Romans knew
in their lifetime. How often the mundane
& bureaucratic lead to accidental wonder,
our best ideas occurring when doing
something else. Gutenberg thinks you're
overthinking this. And Martin Luther
never actually used a nail to affix his
reformation, but nonetheless he still
wanted to show the whole town, church,
world some theses he thought up so they
might remember, even if/when he was
forgotten. Maybe this handy MapQuest
printout will get us there. GPS—what's
the term for mental acuity?—refrigerator
calendars, watches, monuments, Google
reminders, fee schedules, actuarial tables,

menstrual cycle apps, Post-It Notes for
the *loveya & be-right-back*, as if chicken
scratch can tell her how you truly feel.
Torn between going with the flow &
trying to convince the world to see it
as you see it. A red yarn from Aristotle
to Madame Curie to the childhood friend
whose death still has you shook & likely
always will, at least until it's your turn to be
waked. Bookmarks & poems & anthologies
& sheaves & reams & scrolls & libraries
& archives & card catalogue cabinets barely
distinguishable from an apothecary's curio,
as if there's an elixir that's just the tonic
you've been searching for. Microfiche
& the purple-blue wet smell of fresh
mimeographs & special museum taxonomic
cupboards. No matter the Betamax or fax
machine, Sputnik or smartphone, action
is still the clearest form of communication,
so what exactly are the rules governing
this latest competition? Let's consult this
well-organized three-inch binder. The
ultimate game of taking my ball & going
home—the ball = their memories, our shared
adventures, an unrecoverable hard drive
no matter how much rice you soak it in.
You can't unburn those books, but you
can *not* ban them in the first place, their
reconstructed ashes flimsier than water
as they slip through your fingers, dust
to dust, figments on the wind, back into
Earth's surly bonds. And this is exactly why
it hurts so much to lose the ones you love.

Mnemonic Device for the Periodic Table of Elements

First column first box is one wife,
in bed & naked, except for socks,
green & not inert. She's also neon
& carbon & titanium & helium.
Never travel without your own
pillow because the seven wonders
of the modern or ancient world look
a lot less full of wonder with a crick
in your neck. When you wonder
about the last time you brushed
your teeth, at least mix in a breathmint,
or coffee, or gosh even cesium or
tobacco, one of the primary deodorants
for several centuries. Nosegays &
boutonnieres. Cobalt, potassium,
& calcium. Tomato/tomato. The laws
of causality perpetually at odds with the
laws of loss. [Piano solo] because
your music memory has rarely-if-ever
disappointed you, even when the facts
of your chemical composition have.
Just how lucky are you to live not during
the Agricultural, Industrial, or French
Revolutions, but yes instead during
the Dunning-Kruger Epoch? When did
the Great Books Revolution devolve
 into the Great Guns Revolution?
Magnesium, tungsten, & radium.
Featuring *tsk tsk* tsar impersonating
propogandists on your parent's news
network. Noble gasses defined as
such because they aren't trapped
in a bedrock of ignorance, the era
where guns not libraries are repositories
for memories, cultural advancement,
& there's nothing like cuddling up
with your Earl Gray, cat, & a warm gun.
Bismuth, bromide, & other exotic extracts.

Guns are how the pope is chosen.
Guns are a spouse of decades. Yes,
you're upset she passed away—
arsenic & sulfur & lead—but
maybe more upset that half your
memory went with her. Hey, can
you hold this for me? It's best not
to ask questions. [Saxophone solo]:
Outside the street's on fire in a real death waltz
between what's flesh and what's fantasy
and the poets down here
don't write nothing at all
they just stand back and let it all be
and in the quick of the night they reach for their moment
and try to make an honest stand
but they wind up wounded, not even dead.
Dearly departed or maybe just wounded,
be careful about what you really want
to know, as not just anyone can rise to meet
their maximum level of incompetence,
our reasons for needing reasons
always changing. Causes that
give us a because always evolving.
And over the course of two nights
my wife sleeptalked *I'm NOT going to*
climb that fence & *Why am I the assistant?*
Just hold it, honey. I thought I requested
respectfully: don't ask questions. So when
are we going to accept, finally, that these
horizontal relationships are better for us
than the ladder of vertical ones? If you
can't climb anymore, just get off. Drift-fall
with the rest of past project paint chips
flaking onto the windshield of my
commute to campus is an hour of
flat Ohio highway struggling to rise
from its radon & too red rust & I know
if I could instead point the hood ornament
up, vertical, I'd arrive in space at just about
the same time. But there's no comparison.
Because there's little compassion left

when you turn every memory game
into a competition. Game board once
again overturned. And hierarchies,
unlike revolutions, when not elemental,
mostly always do more harm than good.
Unlike oxygen. Yep, exactly unlike oxygen.

Notes, Acknowledgments, & Gratitude for *And/Or*

I.
This Might Be the Spring She Finally Eats Our Lilac Tree
+ Inspired by *The Hidden Life of Trees: What They Feel, How They Communicate* by Peter Wohlleben (2016), "Hills Like White Elephants" by Ernest Hemmingway (1927), "45 Mercy Street" by Anne Sexton (1974), "Mercy Street" by Peter Gabriel (1986), *Water Lilies* by Claude Monet (1915-1926), & "Flowering Judas" by Katherine Anne Porter (1935).
+ Published in *Lean and Loafe: A Journal for New Ecopoetry*, August 2023.

Assume Brilliance
+ Inspired by *The Bassoon King: Art, Idiocy, and Other Sordid Tales from the Band Room* by Rainn Wilson (2015), "If You Knew" by Ellen Bass (2007), *Fire Weather: A True Story From A Hotter World* by John Vaillant (2023), *Fire: A Brief History* by Stephen J. Pyne (2001), The *Pyrocene: How We Created an Age of Fire, and What Happens Next* by Stephen J. Pyne (2021), *Prometheus Bound* by Aeschylus (479BC), "Ozymandias" by Percy Bysshe Shelley (1818), & "Hurt" by Johnny Cash (2002).

The Precision Test's Success
+ Inspired by *The Perfectionists: How Precision Engineers Created the Modern World* by Simon Winchester (2018), "One Train May Hide Another" by Kenneth Koch (1994), *King Lear* by William Shakespeare (1606), & *Frankenstein* by Mary Shelley (1818).
+ Published n *Lean and Loafe: A Journal for New Ecopoetry*, August 2023.

When the Atlantic Ocean is Gone in 170 Million Years, Where Are You Going to Fish?
+ Inspired by Atlantic: *A Vast Ocean of a Million Stories* by Simon Winchester (2010), *The Tempest* by William Shakespeare (1611), & *Quiet: The Power of Introverts in a World That Can't Stop Talking* by Susan Cain (2012).
+ Published in *Metachrosis Literary*, Issue 2, August 1, 2023.

They Were Only Invented in 1947, But There Are Now More Transistors on Earth Than There Are Leaves on Trees
+ Inspired by *The Perfectionists: How Precision Engineers Created the Modern World* by Simon Winchester (2018), T*he Men Who United the States: America's Explorers, Inventors, Eccentrics and Mavericks, and the Creation of One Nation, Indivisible* by Simon Winchester (2013), & "The Locust Tree in Flower" by William Carlos Williams (1935).
+ Published in *The Daily Drunk*, July 5, 2023.

In Australia, Fast Zombies Are Called Zoombies
+ Inspired by *World War Z* (2013), *The Last of Us* (2023), & *The Body Artist* by Don DeLillo (2001).
+ Published n *Lean and Loafe: A Journal for New Ecopoetry*, August 2023.

Rules Are Rules—Until Necessity Intercedes
+ Inspired by *Operation Shylock: A Confession* by Philip Roth (1993), *Crack in the Edge of the World: America and the Great California Earthquake of 1906* by Simon Winchester (2005), & SNL, Season 25, "Celebrity Jeopardy," 1999.
+ Published in *The Hooghly Review*, Issue 2, October 15, 2023.
+ Nominated for a Pushcart Prize.

Time & Rockets & Opposites
+ Inspired by *Gravity's Rainbow* by Thomas Pynchon (1973) & *The Son of Man* by René Magritte (1946).
+ Published in *The Gorko Gazette*, March 18, 2024.

Stephen Jay Gould's Peripatetic Circus
+ Inspired by *Ulysses* by James Joyce (1922), *Dinosaur in a Haystack* by Stephen Jay Gould (1995), & *Hoover: An Extraordinary Life in Extraordinary Times* by Kenneth Whyte (2017).
+ Published in *Metachrosis Literary*, June 2024.

Of the First 40 Pilots for Air Mail, Only 9 Didn't Crash & Die
+ Inspired by *20 Hours, 40 Min: Our Flight in the Friendship* by Amelia Earhart (1928), *Amelia Earhart: The Sky's No Limit (American Heroes)* by Lori Van Pelt (2005), *Fly Girls: How*

Five Daring Women Defied All Odds and Made Aviation History by Keith O'Brien (2018), *East to the Dawn: The Life of Amelia Earhart* by Susan Butler (1997), "Learning to Fly" by Tom Petty (1991), *Electra* by Sophocles (420BC), *Great Circle* by Maggie Shipstead (2021), "Ode to the West Wind" by Percy Bysshe Shelley (1820), & *The Making of the Atomic Bomb* by Richard Rhodes (1986).
+ Published in *The Gorko Gazette's Amelia Earhart Special*, December 1, 2023.

II.
Chez Jean-Paul: A Three-Star Michelin Journal of Poetry & Pâté Can Suck It

+ Inspired by *Critics, Monsters, Fanatics, and Other Literary Essays* by Cynthia Ozick (2016), Mao II by Don DeLillo (1991), *Catcher in the Rye* by J.D. Salinger (1951), *Lunch Poems* by Frank O'Hara (1964), & *Night at the Museum* (2006).
+ Published in *La Piccioletta Barca*, March 8, 2024.

It's Not That I Fear Seeing a Ghost, But That I Fear Not Seeing One When Everyone Else Does

+ Inspired by *The Turn of the Screw* by Henry James (1898), *The Truth at the Heart of the Lie: How the Catholic Church Lost Its Soul* by James Carroll (2021), & "Design" by Robert Frost (1916).

Mothers of America! Please Let Your Children Come Visit Cleveland!

+ Inspired by "Ave Maria" by Frank O'Hara (1964), *My Favorite Murder Podcast, A Christmas Story* (1983), & "Sonnet 130" by William Shakespeare (1609).
+ Published in *Words & Sports Quarterly,* Volume 2, Issue 4, April 28, 2023.

I Went to a Cake Shoppe Specifically Because It Was Called SLICES, But They Only Sold Whole Cakes

+ Inspired by "The Red Wheelbarrow" by William Carlos Williams (1923) & *The Professor and the Madman: A Tale of Murder, Insanity, and the Making of the Oxford English Dictionary* by Simon Winchester (1998).
+ Published in *Olney Magazine*, Issue 5, May 22, 2023.

The Night I Met Reincarnated Andy Warhol at Bonnie's Bar & Grill in Fairview Park, Ohio
+ Published in *JAKE*, April 27, 2024.

Promise Adventure
+ Published in *The Gorko Gazette's Amelia Earhart Special*, December 1, 2023.

Bomb City
+ Published in T*he Gorko Gazette's American Cheese Special*, May 13, 2023.

Situation: There's a Pint of Ben & Jerry's in Your Freezer. How Many Nights Does It Last?
+Inspired by *Family Feud* (with Richard Dawson), 1976-1985, *How to Stop Time* by Matt Haig (2017), & *Rain Wilson and the Geography of Bliss* (2023).
+ Published in *LEON Literary Review*, December 2023.
+ Nominated for a Pushcart Prize.

III.
Global Flavor Riot
+ Inspired by T*he Taste of Empire: How Britain's Quest for Food Shaped the Modern World* by Lizzie Collingham (2017), *The Taste of Conquest: The Rise and Fall of the Three Great Cities of Spice* by Michael Krondl (2008), *An Edible History of Humanity* by Tom Standage (2009), *Flavor: The Science of Our Most Neglected Sense* by Bob Holmes(2017), *Delicious: The Evolution of Flavor and How It Made Us Human* by Rob R. Dunn (2022), *Science and Cooking: Physics Meets Food, From Homemade to Haute* Cuisine by Michael Brenner (2020), *Kitchen Confidential: Adventures in the Culinary Underbelly* by Anthony Bourdain (2000), *This Land is Their Land: The Wampanoag Indians, Plymouth Colony, and the Troubled History of Thanksgiving* by David J. Silverman (2019), "Don't Stop Believin'" by Journey (1981), "Hollaback Girl" by Gwen Sefani (2016), *The Jungle* by Upton Sinclair (1906),"Kubla Kahn" by Samuel Taylor Coleridge (1797), "The Lottery" by Shirley Jackson (1948), "We Built This City" by Starship (1985), "The Yada Yada," Seinfeld, Season 8, Episode 19 (1997), "Watermelon Sugar" by Harry Styles (2019), *King Lear* by William Shakespeare (1608), "Wannabe" by Spice Girls (1996),

"Instant Karma! (We All Shine On)" by John Lennon & Yoko Ono (1970), "Pumpkin Spice: The Science Behind the Invasion. Plus, What's the Next Big Flavor Fad?" Every Little Thing Podcast, (December 10, 2018), "One Train May Hide Another Train" by Kenneth Koch (1994), & "Paul's Case" by Willa Cather (1905).
+ Published in *Erato Magazine,* June 1, 2023.

IV.
When I Finally Began Talking to Myself In Sir David Attenborough's Voice
+ Inspired by *Prehistoric Planet*, Apple TV (2022-2023), *Great Expectations* by Charles Dickens (1861), & *Brief Candle in the Dark* by Richard Dawkins (2015).
+ Published in *LEON Literary Review,* December 2023.

Wax Management
+ Published in *Full House Literary: The Games Room,* March 2023.

The Opposite of Anthropomorphic
+ Inspired by Ross Gay's "Fireflies"(2019).
+ Published in *The Gorko Gazette's American Cheese Special,* May 13, 2023.

The Age Where I Need to Take a Photo & Then Zoom In, In Order to Read the Fine Print
+ Inspired by *Where Are We Heading: The Evolution of Humans and Things* by Ian Hodder (2018), *The Psychopath Test: A Journey Through the Madness Industry* by Jon Ronson (2011), "Dan Gilbert: The Surprising Science of Happiness" TED Talk (2014), & *Natural Rivals: John Muir, Gifford Pinchot, and the Creation of America's Public Lands* by John Clayton (2019).
+ Published in *Gone Lawn*, Issue 50, Buck Moon, July 2, 2023.

Because the Weather Changes
+ Published in *Gone Lawn*, Issue 50, Buck Moon, July 2, 2023.

Think About All the Things You're Not Thinking About
+ Published in *Words & Sports Quarterly*, Volume 2, Issue 4, April 28, 2023.

I'm Late to It, but Here's a Review of James Cameron's Humongous, Gigantic Blockbuster, Avatar: the Way of Water (2022)
+ Published in *coalitionworks*, May 12, 2023.

When Will You Stop Trying to Live Up to the Length of Your Own Shadow?
+ Published in *Blue Flame Review,* Issue 1: Tessellate, June 15, 2023.

A Self-Perpetuating Cycle of Self-Perpetuation
+ Inspired by "Big Shot" by Billy Joel (1978), "Fight For Your Right" by Beastie Boys (1986), *Wizard: the Life and Times of Nikola Tesla* by Marc Seifer (1996), & *Tides: The Science and Spirit of the Ocean* by Jonathan White (2017).
+ Published in *coalitionworks*, May 12, 2023.

The Time I Brought a Vase Half-filled with Water to Bed
+ Published in *The Hooghly Review*, Issue 2, October 15, 2023.

V.
On Becoming My 75-Year-Old Mother's Medical Marijuana Plug
+ Published in *Fahmidan Journal*, Issue 16, June 20, 2023.

Sometimes You Don't Know You're in a Bubble Until It Pops
+ Inspired by *How to Do the Work: Recognize Your Patterns, Heal from Your Past, and Create Your Self* by Dr. Nicole LePera (2021), *One Fish, Two Fish, Red Fish, Blue Fish* by Dr. Seuss (1960), & "Bulls on Parade" by Rage Against the Machine (1996).

Terminal Uniqueness
+ Inspired by *Christ the Redeemer* by Paul Landowski (1931), *The Republic* by Plato (375 BC), & *Pale Blue Dot* by Carl Sagan (1994).

Anxiety Mascot
+ Inspired by "The Rocking-Horse Winner" by D.H. Lawrence (1925) & *Fuzz: When Nature Breaks the Law* by Mary Roach (2021).
+ Published in *Words & Sports Quarterly*, Volume 2, Issue 4, April 28, 2023.

It's Magic, When Folks Don't See the Science Behind It
+ Published in *Moss Puppy Magazine*, Issue 4: Caged, May 11, 2023.

Everyone is Walking Along—Floating Along—& You're the One with a Stone in Your Shoe

Sofia the Flying Telescope
+ Inspired by *The Last Stargazers: The Enduring Story of Astronomy's Vanishing Explorers* by Emily Levesque (2020) & *The Pregnant Widow* by Martin Amis (2010).
+ Published *The Gorko Gazette*, February 27, 2024.

Ignorance of the Present
+ Inspired by *Harry S. Truman: A Life* by Robert H. Ferrell (1994) & *David Copperfield* by Charles Dickens (1850).
+ Published *The Gorko Gazette*, March 18, 2024.

Burning Birds & Fiery Jets: Mayday Mayday Mayday is French for Help Me
+ Inspired by: Britain's Got Talent (2007) & America's Got Talent (2006-), *A Season On The Wind: Inside the World of Spring Migration* by Kenn Kaufman (2019), "Angel" by Sarah McLaughlin (1997), *Hamlet* by William Shakespeare (1603), *Neil Armstrong: A Life of Flight* by Jay Barbee (2014), *The Colossus of New York* by Colson Whitehead (2003), *Brave New World* by Aldous Huxley (1932), & "The Emperor of Ice Cream" by Wallace Stevens (1954).
+ Published in *The Gorko Gazette*, February 27, 2024.

The Archeology of the Ampersand
+ Published in *Rabble Review,* Issue 7, October 20, 2023.

VI.
There's Documented Evidence of Telegraph Operators in the Distant & Almost Completely Isolated Operation Stations of the American Southwest Falling in Love, Despite the Century Beginning With 18, the Tumbleweeds, the Single Iron Wire, Poles Impersonating Cacti, Dots, Dashes, Omissions, Hesitations, False Starts, & At-First- Unobvious- Yet-Still-Horrific Anti-Indigenous Propaganda

+ Inspired by *The Victorian Internet: The Remarkable Story of the Telegraph and the Nineteenth Century's On-line Pioneers* by Tom Standage (1998), *Land: How the Hunger for Ownership Shaped the Modern World* by Simon Winchester (2021), & "Having a Coke with You" by Frank O'Hara (1960).
+ Published in *Drunk Monkeys,* Volume 8, Number 5, May 15, 2023.

Well, Well, Well… As If It Isn't the Consequences of My Own Actions

I Always Thought That Elton John Song Went, "Hold Me Closer, Tony Danza…."

+ Inspired by "Tiny Dancer" by Elton John (1971), *Ninth Street Women: Lee Krasner, Elaine de Kooning, Grace Hartigan, Joan Mitchell, and Helen Frankenthaler: Five Painters and the Movement That Changed Modern Art* by Mary Gabriel (2018),& *Rin Tin Tin: The Life and the Legend* by Susan Orlean (2011).
+ Published in *The Hooghly Review,* Issue 2, October 15, 2023.

Like Frogs Around a Pond

+ Inspired by *The Lessons of History* by Will & Ariel Durant (1968), W*ho We Are and How We Got Here: Ancient DNA and the New Science of the Human Past* by David Reich (2018), & *Phaedo* by Plato (360 BC).
+ Published in *Blue Flame Review,* Issue 1: Tessellate, June 15, 2023.

How to Cultivate Political Propaganda

+ Inspired by C*affeine: How Caffeine Created the Modern World* by Michael Pollan (2020) & *Alice's Adventures in Wonderland* by Lewis Carroll (1865).

**How Often We Store Our Memories
Outside Our Minds**
> \+ Inspired by *Knowing What We Know: The Transmission of Knowledge: From Ancient Wisdom to Modern Magic* by Simon Winchester (2023), *A Bend in the River* by V.S. Naipaul (1979). & *The Man from the Train: The Solving of a Century-Old Serial Killer Mystery* by Bill James and Rachel McCarthy James (2017).

Mnemonic Device for the Periodic Table of Elements
> \+ Inspired by "Jungleland" by Bruce Springsteen (1975), "How the Pope is Chosen" by James Tate (1994), *Algorithms to Live By: The Computer Science of Human Decisions* by Brian Christian and Tom Griffiths (2016), & *The Courage to Be Disliked: The Japanese Phenomenon That Shows You How to Change Your Life and Achieve Real Happiness* by Ichiro Kishimi and Fumitake Koga (2013).
> \+ Published in *Don't Submit!* March 24, 2023.

Thank you to all of my family, friends, & colleagues—for all of your love & support. Thank you also, especially, to Jessica Jones, Ankit Raj Ojha, & everyone at Finishing Line Press.

Bob King is a Professor of English at Kent State University at Stark & has taught at KSU for 27 years, winning multiple teaching distinctions. He holds degrees from Loyola University Chicago & Indiana University (MFA, poetry), where he was Editor of *Indiana Review*. He's a recipient of an Ohio Arts Council Individual Artist Fellowship & part of a team that won a 2023-2024 National Endowment for the Arts / Arts Midwest Big Read Communities Grant. He lives in Fairview Park, Ohio, with his wife & daughters.

www.ingramcontent.com/pod-product-compliance
Lightning Source LLC
Chambersburg PA
CBHW031435150426
43191CB00006B/526